Soccer Training Programs

Gerhard Frank

# Soccer Training Programs

Meyer & Meyer Sports

Original title: Trainingsprogramme Fußball
© Meyer & Meyer Verlag Aachen
Translated by Paul D. Chilvers-Grierson

British Library Cataloguing in Publication Data
A catalogue record for this book is available from the British Library

**Soccer Training Programs**
Maidenhead: Meyer & Meyer Sport (UK) Ltd., 1999
2nd Edition 2009
ISBN: 978-1-84126-274-1

© 1999 by Meyer & Meyer Sport (UK) Ltd.
2nd Edition 2009
Aachen, Adelaide, Auckland, Budapest, Cape Town, Graz,
Indianapolis, Maidenhead, Olten (CH), Singapore, Toronto
Member of the World
Sports Publishers' Association (WSPA)
www.w-s-p-a.org

Printed and bound by: B.O.S.S Druck und Medien GmbH, Germany
ISBN: 978-1-84126-274-1
E-Mail: info@m-m-sports.com
www.m-m-sports.com

# Contents

**Foreword** . . . . . . . . . . . . . . . . . . . . . . . . . . . . . . . . . . . . . . . . . . .**7**

**1**   **Introduction** . . . . . . . . . . . . . . . . . . . . . . . . . . . . . . . . . . .**9**

**2**   **General Training Approaches** . . . . . . . . . . . . . . . . . . . . . . . . .**11**
   The Significance of Fitness . . . . . . . . . . . . . . . . . . . . . . . . . . . . . . . . . .11
   Definitions . . . . . . . . . . . . . . . . . . . . . . . . . . . . . . . . . . . . . . . . . . .12

**3**   **Psychological Aspects (Mental Behavior)** . . . . . . . . . . . . . . . . . . .**15**

**4**   **Training Principles Peculiar to Soccer** . . . . . . . . . . . . . . . . . . . . .**17**
   Training Forms . . . . . . . . . . . . . . . . . . . . . . . . . . . . . . . . . . . . . . . .19
   – Strength Training (Muscle Training) . . . . . . . . . . . . . . . . . . . . . . . . . . .20
   – Speed Training . . . . . . . . . . . . . . . . . . . . . . . . . . . . . . . . . . . . . . .21
   – Endurance Training . . . . . . . . . . . . . . . . . . . . . . . . . . . . . . . . . . . .22
   Training Methods for Endurance . . . . . . . . . . . . . . . . . . . . . . . . . . . . . .23

**5**   **Techniques and Tactics in Amateur Soccer** . . . . . . . . . . . . . . . . . . .**25**

**6**   **Training Periods and Planning** . . . . . . . . . . . . . . . . . . . . . . . . . . .**28**

**7**   **Organisational Tips** . . . . . . . . . . . . . . . . . . . . . . . . . . . . . . . . . .**32**

**8**   **Performance Measurement** . . . . . . . . . . . . . . . . . . . . . . . . . . . . .**32**

**9**   **Explanation of Symbols** . . . . . . . . . . . . . . . . . . . . . . . . . . . . . . .**34**

**10**   **Training Programs** . . . . . . . . . . . . . . . . . . . . . . . . . . . . . . . . . . .**35**

**11**   **Training in Halls and Fitness Studios** . . . . . . . . . . . . . . . . . . . . . .**192**
   Circuit Program Tailored to Soccer . . . . . . . . . . . . . . . . . . . . . . . . . . . .193
   Training in the Fitness Studio . . . . . . . . . . . . . . . . . . . . . . . . . . . . . . . .194

**12**   **Appendix – Stretching** . . . . . . . . . . . . . . . . . . . . . . . . . . . . . . . .**203**

Photo & Illustration Credits . . . . . . . . . . . . . . . . . . . . . . . . . . . . . . . . . . . . .213

# Foreword

Since publication of the first edition (1978) there have been rapid developments in soccer. This is reflected in a growing number of publications which deal with the changed conditions and problems in professional and amateur soccer.

In particular the aspect of training, i.e. planning, structure and frequency, has been covered increasingly extensively. In the past 20 years the emphasis in training has been placed on fitness and tactical elements. Amateur soccer also seemed to profit from general developments in professional soccer and often training content and goals were transferred unquestioningly to the amateur field without sufficient consideration of structural differences here.

Technique and creativity often received too little attention. The purpose of this fifth edition is therefore, under a new title, to place the area of technique more in the foreground of training planning. Reflecting changes in the yearly rhythm – winter break and bad field conditions are now also a feature in amateur soccer – a chapter on "Training in halls and fitness studios" has been added.

Numerous photos and diagrams are designed to make daily use of the programs easier.

My special thanks go to the publisher Meyer & Meyer Sport which has made this heavily revised new edition possible. The author thanks the demonstrators Spend Madjouni, Martin Kretzer and Phillip Lippert for their cooperation for the photos, and the company adidas for providing the sports and training clothing.

We wish all trainers and instructors success and enjoyment in their work in amateur soccer.

*Gerhard Frank*

# 1   Introduction

High performance sport in soccer is marked by high demands on participants and trainers in both the professional and the amateur fields.

Modern soccer calls for the highest degree of commitment, willingness and concentration on the part of all involved in order to meet fitness and tactical performance demands.

In addition players must develop characteristics such as stamina, resilience, fast reactions, sociability, and strong nerves.

Some of these characteristics are natural, others can be developed with appropriate training. It is therefore the trainer's task to promote and improve not only the physical but also the mental strengths of his players. Individual talks but also teamwork are the best methods.

Adequate time should be devoted to the training of tactics in addition to technique, but without over-emphasising complicated moves in theory and practice. Technique and fitness come first so that players can keep up with the fast pace of the game.

The rapid development towards a game based on speed must be reflected in a corresponding training form.

The exact training planning must consider on the one hand the annual rhythm, but also the weekly matches with their varying demands on players. Training as such is a holistic process, marked by a balance of strain and rest.

Amateur soccer not only means performance sport on a broad basis. These days it also often means commercialization down to the lowest divisions, payment for players who change clubs, bonuses to players for wins, dependence on supporting firms and sponsors. That frequently means lucrative offers in the junior levels and thus a draining of smaller clubs and with this resignation and stagnation in junior soccer.

In contrast to professional soccer, amateur soccer must often struggle with unsatisfactory external factors. Optimum training conditions are seldom found. Poor quality fields, lack of floodlighting, insufficient training material such as balls, skipping ropes, slalom poles, etc. make the trainer's job harder.

The trainer must be prepared for lack of interest on the part of the players, but also for a variety of influences from family and occupational circles. Constant work over a complete season or even over several years is often made difficult or impossible. In the amateur field too, the trainer's commitment is also determined by success and failure. The success of his work is therefore dependent on the factors around him.

For this reason it is important to make training varied and exciting in order to motivate players again and again.

Many trainers and coaches in amateur soccer do not have enough time to devise their own training plans. These training programs can support the coach in his work, whereby he should always check them for their suitability to his needs and adapt them if necessary. They are therefore just a framework to support the trainer's own ideas, allowing him optimal use of his time and providing him with additional input to realise his own concepts.

# 2 General Training Approaches

The purpose of this brief introduction to general training approaches is to provide basic knowledge of the composition of training structures.

By training we mean long term systematic building up of a sportsperson or team to their highest level of sporting ability.

Training correctly carried out is therefore a uniform process which should improve both the physical aspects of endurance, strength, speed, flexibility, coordination and skill as well as the psychological aspects of sensitivity, strength of will, self control, courage, drive, and decisiveness.

In the course of the training process there will always be adaptations of the whole organism to the increased performance level. The heart and circulatory system, the central nervous system, metabolism, muscles, tendons, ligaments and joints all play a decisive role, which can also place limits on performance.

Good physical fitness for sports can only be achieved when the physical and the psychological (mental-spiritual) aspects are harmonised with each other.

A player who enters the field without the internal willingness to do his best will most certainly not reach his best level of performance; he will also never be able to satisfyingly fulfill the tactical tasks assigned to him.

On the other hand, the "super technician" who is not fit will not be able to make use of his abilities for the full 90 minutes.

## The Significance of Fitness

By fitness we mean a condition of physical ability to perform which is marked by both physical and mental factors. The physical ability to perform (fitness) consists of various elements:

Strength

Endurance

Speed

Suppleness/Agility

Skill/Coordination

# Definitions

**Endurance:** The body's resistance to tiredness when the whole body is moving, over as long a time as possible, e.g. cycling, long-distance running, swimming.

The term endurance can be segmented according to different types of strain.

By general endurance the inclusion of as many groups of muscles as possible during a sporting activity is meant. Localised endurance on the other hand is restricted to a certain group of muscles, e.g. the arm.

**Endurance is dependent:**
a) On the quality of the heart and circulatory systems (intake and processing of oxygen).
b) On the metabolic processes (provision and release of energy).
c) On the central nervous system.

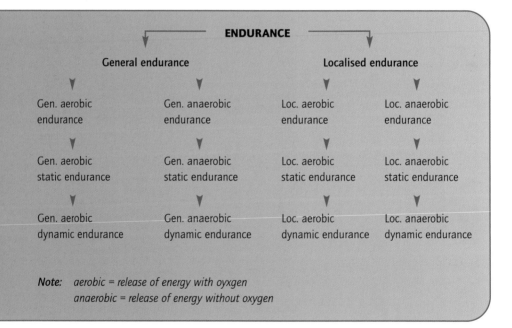

|  | ENDURANCE | | |
|---|---|---|---|
| **General endurance** | | **Localised endurance** | |
| Gen. aerobic endurance | Gen. anaerobic endurance | Loc. aerobic endurance | Loc. anaerobic endurance |
| Gen. aerobic static endurance | Gen. anaerobic static endurance | Loc. aerobic static endurance | Loc. anaerobic static endurance |
| Gen. aerobic dynamic endurance | Gen. anaerobic dynamic endurance | Loc. aerobic dynamic endurance | Loc. anaerobic dynamic endurance |

*Note:* aerobic = release of energy with oyxgen
anaerobic = release of energy without oxygen

**Strength:** The ability of the muscular system to contract against resistance without the base and the origin of the muscle on the particular bone section coming together (isometric method). Strength is also overcoming one's own body weight (the muscle shortens = concentric method).

**Motor strength is determined by:**

a) the composition and structure of the muscles (cross-section of muscle fibre, fast or slow twitching fibre),

b) the contraction speed of the muscle and its coordination with the central nervous system (creation and transmission of impulses).

**There are various forms of strength:**

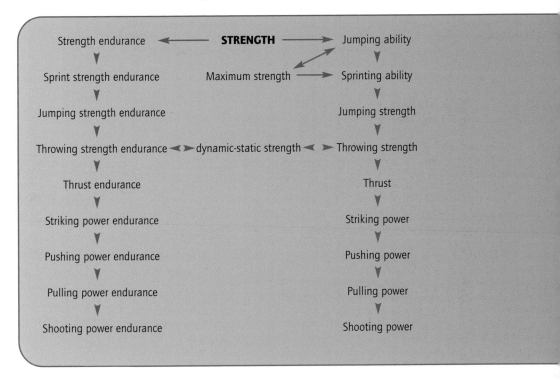

**Speed:** The ability to carry out movements at high velocity, e.g. sprint. The following is decisive for the speed of a movement:

a) Composition of muscle fibres (fast or slow twitching),

b) Coordination of muscle and nervous system,

c) Release of energy in the muscle cell,

d) Elasticity of muscle fibres,

e) Ability of the muscle to relax.

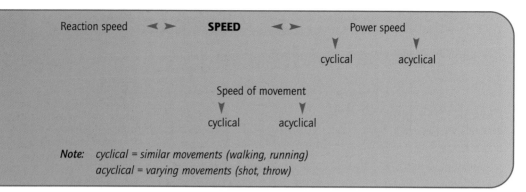

Note:   cyclical = similar movements (walking, running)
acyclical = varying movements (shot, throw)

**Suppleness/Agility:** The ability to make use of the joints' movement options in all directions (breadth of movement).

**Suppleness is dependent on:**
a)  The elasticity of muscles, tendons, ligaments,
b)  Muscle tension,
c)  Factors of age (menstruation cycle, hormonal situation),
d)  Psychological factors (mood, motivation),
e)  Other factors (time of day, climate, temperature).

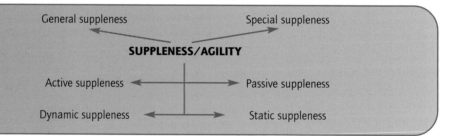

### Skill/Coordination
Skill/coordination are the interaction of the central nervous system and the muscle system within a movement process. We can differentiate between intramuscular and intermuscular coordination:

**Intramuscular coordination** is the nerve-muscle interaction of a single muscle during a specific movement.

**Intermuscular coordination** is the interaction of various muscles during a specific movement.

# 3 Psychological Aspects (Mental Behavior)

If a player is to be taken to the limits of his sporting capability one must attend not only to general and particular aspects of fitness, but must also influence his performing behavior and in doing so always take into consideration his personal needs.

Knowing about the player's social environment (family background, own family, school, working life), his habits and any health problems helps the trainer to exactly judge his abilities at any given time.

He can thus specifically and positively influence the player's training effort and motivation. Reaching optimum sporting fitness is of course first and foremost dependent on the entire personality structure of the player, – i.e. on his strength of will and drive, self control, unselfishness and readiness for action, but also on moods and influences determined by his upbringing.

Every trainer should therefore match and utilise the varying temperaments in his team both during and outside training.

Briefly, we can characterise three groups of player types:
a) the introverted player (schizothyme) who is inhibited and self-conscious and lives under constant psychological tension;
b) the extroverted player (cyclothyme) who is easily irritated and explodes for the slightest reason, complains, gesticulates;
c) the so-called robust type who is secure in himself, stands up to psychological pressure even in difficult situations, stays "cool," in fact "the" player personality.

Players and trainer should be aware that for keeping to tactical concepts, for planning and for comprehension of playing actions, thinking processes are required which are directed from the cerebral cortex.

Feelings too, such as fear, fright, anger, rage and joy, which every player experiences in the course of a game, are based in the cerebral trunk and are influenced by the release of the hormones adrenalin and noradrenalin.

Depending on the combination of the two hormones there can be a blocking of consciousness by rage, fury, anger (noradrenalin) or an increase of consciousness and ability to react more quickly (adrenalin).

It is thus clear that certain actions in a competitive match are considerably influenced by personal psychological conditions of tension and excitability.

These conditions include:
- Fear of making a fool of oneself in front of team-mates, friends, spectators, of losing one's regular place, etc.
- Disappointment (frustration) when goals were set too high (championship, cup success); when one had believed a victory was certain; at insufficient playing opportunities.
- Tiredness, when fitness level sinks; when the subjective performance limit has been reached.
- Feelings of inferiority when one cannot cope with fitness, technique and tactical aspects; through lack of recognition by one's own team.
- Oversaturation, through uniformity of strain in training; too many matches or tournaments; due to repetitive reactions and instructions from the trainer.
- Expectations of oneself and others, when external expectations are too high (club, team-mates, media); lack of ability to estimate one's own performance capacity.

It is the trainer's job to deal with individual players during training and channel emotionally driven behavior into concentrated behavior.

The player must be convinced that only emotionally free behavior can lead to success.

This change of behavior is best carried out in personal conversations with the trainer or individual team members.

For the all important team building process, in which the individual players learn to be group members and get used to acting as a team, it is essential that all players are psychologically in a good state of mind.

A stable mental situation also contributes to successfully dealing with the manifold psychological and social conflicts that can arise in a team, the most significant of which are:
- varying willingness to contribute,
- sport and work,
- family problems,
- sexual needs,
- attitude to competition,
- fear of injury,
- personal insecurity,
- questioning the point of organised sport,
- age and generation differences between players and trainer.

# 4 Training Principles Peculiar to Soccer

The special demands of amateur training can best be solved with a specific training approach. The various training types and methods with their differing structures must be coordinated with each other.

The resulting training strain arises from the amount and the intensity of training, which must be in a sensible proportion to one another.

The amount and intensity of training, however, only allow a rough guide to long-term planning of training.

Strain and adaptation can be explained as a process of stimulus and reaction. A subliminal stimulus will not lead to adaptation, one that is too intensive causes over training.

Not only the stimuli must be taken into consideration when planning the amount of training, but also the variation between strain and recovery.

The associated development of the training situation is based on the principle of "super compensation," i.e. the energy used up by the strain must be built up again by the organism.

Every training stimulus leads to a decrease in energy rich substances, which in itself is already a stimulus to build them up again. The recovery phase should not, however, last until the beginning value of the previous strain is reached, but should start earlier with a renewed movement stimulus (see Fig. 1).

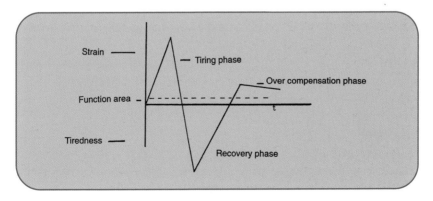

*Fig. 1: The Principle of Super Compensation (Source: FRANK, G.: Training Programme für Fußball-Amateurvereine, 4th Ed. 1988)*

The following is a brief description of some other training principles with validity for soccer.

The principle of **increasing the strain** reflects a constant improvement of training and match performance. The improvement is linear (e.g. beginners' training) or progressive (advanced training) or in steps and with increasing tiredness (high performance training).

The principle of **permanence** and non-seasonality says that the training process is regular and without major breaks.

The principle of **maximum strain** means that the relationship between strain and breaks must be harmonious so that restoration processes – short ones in seconds and minutes (building up of energy rich phosphates) – long ones in hours or days (building up of carbohydrate stores and protein structures) are ensured.

The principle of **variation of strain** involves a skillful combining of different training goals and methods to allow for flexibility and variability in the area of technique in particular.

The principle of **periodization** helps the trainer to maintain stability of form and to prevent loss of form.

The principle of **individualization** aims at training tailored to the individual player. This is certainly only possible in top amateur and professional levels.

Decisive for successful training is knowledge of strain characteristics as described below.

It is important to know that the amount and the intensity of strain counter each other, i.e. the greater the amount, the less the intensity and vice versa.

To guarantee a certain dosage of strain, strain criteria must be established. These are: stimulus intensity, stimulus amount, stimulus duration, stimulus density, stimulus frequency and training frequency.

### Stimulus intensity
Stimulus intensity is the strength of the individual stimulus or a series of stimuli, e.g. run as hard as you can or speed dribbling. Movement frequencies such as skipping can be seen as measurements of stimulus intensity.

### Stimulus amount
Stimulus amount describes the duration and the number of stimuli per training unit, the number of repetitions, the sum of the distances covered or also the sum of the weights lifted.

### Stimulus duration
Stimulus duration is the length of time a particular stimulus or a series of stimuli is applied, often the time taken to cover a certain distance.

### Stimulus density
Stimulus density characterises the temporal order of the stimuli and represents the relationship between strain and recovery, e.g. in speed or jumping training there should be complete breaks between the individual stimuli.

### Stimulus frequency
Stimulus frequency describes the number of repetitions or series.

### Trainings frequency
Training frequency indicates the number of training sessions per day or week.

# Training Forms

On the basis of the strain put on the muscle systems one can differentiate between three general forms of training:
1.  Strength training (muscle training)
2.  Speed training
3.  Endurance training

An increase in strength, speed and endurance is achieved by improving the strengths important to each.

Strength or muscle training mainly affects the muscle systems subjected to strain (with soccer players the leg and stomach muscles). An increase in muscle strength is achieved mainly through tensing muscles against strong resistance (e.g. partner or weights). Endurance is best increased with numerous tensings of muscles against slight resistance.

Even if the training types are not interchangeable, they nevertheless have a positive effect on the characteristic trained in each case. Speed depends partially on strength and can thus also be increased by an increase in strength. In a situation of purely speed training, coordination in particular and other conductory and switching processes in the nervous system are improved.

## Strength Training (Muscle Training)

In soccer, strength is required whenever the body mass of the player is moved, with or without the ball. Especially in one on one situations the pulling and holding of arms and jerseys leads to an enormous strain, which is only short, but occurs often.

Strength training particularly encourages growth of the muscles placed under strain. In connection with soccer this means that the strength needed for running, kicking and taking-off is decidedly improved so that it can be applied both for speed and endurance.

In the context of soccer training it therefore makes little sense to merely produce muscle volume through maximum strength training with heavy weights. It is much more effective to favor dynamic muscle training in which the interaction of the muscles, basic speed and speed of movement are all improved simultaneously.

Strength training can also be carried out with the aid of gymnastic exercises when in certain exercises the partner's body weight must be moved.

Dug up or difficult ground leads to increased use of strength both in training and in playing and thus to both improved strength and endurance.

The following forms of exercise are useful for soccer:

1. Strain through external weight (see also chapter "Training in Halls and Fitness Studios"), single weights or dumb-bell machine.
2. Overcoming resistance of a partner (struggle for medicine ball, push and pull competition).
3. Overcoming one's own weight in jumping and holding exercises under the strain of external weights (medicine ball, sand bag, weight vest).
4. Overcoming resistance of partner under strain of external weights (cavalry battle or cavalry soccer).

The level of strain is expressed in per cent of a person's maximum strength, i.e. the person's individual capacity limit in a particular exercise. As a result of the growth in strength this capacity limit moves upwards and therefore has to be gauged again every 14 days.

## Speed Training

During a match speed capabilities are constantly required. Certain game signals call for certain reactions to opponent and ball. These actions take place at top speed, whether it be acceleration with the ball, a sprint man against man or a skillful breakaway over a short distance.

An increase in speed, however, can only be achieved if the factors decisive to speed performance are improved.

Because speed is mainly dependent on basic strength, appropriate dynamic strength training has the effect of improving speed.

Another important means of increasing speed are coordination exercises which lead to faster functioning of the nervous system.

These exercises have an accelerating effect especially on the interaction of the muscles, on reaction time and on the speed at which the muscles contract.

Speed training calls for sufficient breaks  so that the nervous system can completely recover and thus remain fully sensitive to impulses.

In speed training the emphasis can be placed either on speed endurance (playing pace) or resilience.

Speed training should never be carried out using exercises that tire extremely as the training stimuli cannot be fully effective in this case.

The decisive stimuli occur at a high to maximum intensity of movement at full amplitude of the steps. Optimum strength of stimuli are 20 m to 50 m sprints with and without the ball, whereby an appropriate stimulus density must be ensured.

In soccer speed training is very important quite simply because in many situations higher speed, the fast sprint to the ball, the sudden change of direction or the surprise dash past the opponent with the ball can decide the game.

The faster a player reacts, the faster he can start, the sooner he gets possession of the ball and he thus has an enormous advantage in the particular game situation.

## Endurance Training

The great significance of endurance is undisputed in amateur and professional sport. Especially in preparing for the season planned basic endurance training plays a key role.

Constant movement during the game, active reacting with and without the ball tires players as the game goes on. Planned endurance training can help combat this. The often brief but intensive strain situations can be compensated by systematically carried out endurance training – including during the season – which also supports the process of restoration and recovery.

Endurance training can be carried out in the form of forest or cross-country running, or in the form of appropriate exercises with the ball. It is an accepted fact that endurance training with the ball is easier to bear and is more fun for the participants.

Players who are better trained endurance wise are less prone to injuries and thus again and again more quickly reachieve full capacity.

The organism can better process the products of the body's metabolism and more quickly overcome energy bottlenecks.

The endurance trained player is thus more stress resistent and has a higher degree of psychological stability which makes him more able to deal with frustration, defeats and motivation problems.

Endurance training should nevertheless not be carried out for its own sake but should always be seen in regard to soccer.

For the soccer player this means he does not have to improve his endurance ability to maximum levels of excess but rather to better integrate it into the technical and tactical total plan.

Not only general aerobic endurance  is required of the player. Special anaerobic endurance increases physical capacity too. The ability to repeat speed and direction changes, accelerations, headers, goal shots etc. as often as possible during the whole game are characteristics of this special kind of endurance.

*Note:*     *aerobic = energy supply with oxygen*
            *anaerobic = energy supply with development of lactic acid*

# Training Methods for Endurance

In endurance training three forms are accepted:

- Long-term endurance (running at 40-60% of maximum capacity) – the strains are spatially and temporally very long and are interrupted by short walking periods at the most.
  Type of training: Forest or cross-country running.

- Medium-term endurance is improved by running at 60-80% of maximum capacity – the strains last 40 seconds to two minutes with sufficient breaks to make up for the lack of oxygen.
  Type of training: Runs or ball work, e.g. 4:4 with two ball contacts per player.

- Short-term endurance is improved by runs at high speed (75-90% of maximum capacity). The length of strain is short – 15-45 seconds without the ball, with the ball 45-120 seconds. The following complete recovery breaks (3-5 min) can be used actively (light ball work, individually or as a team).
  Type of training: Speed runs over short distances or ball work, e.g. 1:1, 2:2 struggle for the ball.

| RUNNING TRAINING | STRENGTH TRAINING |
|---|---|
| **1. Long-term performance method** | |
| Stimulus strength: 25-75% of max. capacity | Gradually increase |
| Stimulus amount: very large | Very large, gradually increase |
| Stimulus density: Practise without breaks | Practices without breaks |
| Stimulus duration: long – more than 8 minutes | Till complete exhaustion |
| Training effect: Improvement of general endurance capability. | |
| **2. Extensive interval method** | |
| Stimulus strength: 60-80% of max. capacity | 50-60% of max. capacity |
| Stimulus amount: 20-30 repeats | Series with 25 repeats with |
| generous breaks | |
| Stimulus density: Fast repeats, 45-90 s breaks | Fast repeats, 45-90 s breaks |
| Stimulus duration: long – 20-70 s | short (15-30 s) |
| Training effect: Improvement of general respectively strength endurance capability. | |

### 3. Intensive interval method

Stimulus strength: 80-90% of max. capacity          75% of max. capacity
Stimulus amount: 10-12 repeats                      Series with 12 repeats
Stimulus density: lowered (90-180 s breaks)         Lowered (90-180 s breaks)
Stimulus duration: short (4-20 s)                   short (4-20 s)

Training effect: Improvement of speed, endurance capability respectively of strength endurance and speed.

### 4. Repeat method

Stimulus strength: 90-100% of max. capacity         100% of max. capacity
Stimulus amount: 1-3 runs over 100 to 300 m         Series with 3-6 repeats or
20-30 individual exercises
Stimulus density: 10-45 min breaks                  3-5 min breaks
Stimulus duration: short                            short

Training effect: Improvement of speed resp. of maximum and resilience strength.

**Tip:** For all of these training methods stretching before, during and after the exercises is highly recommended.

# 5 Techniques and Tactics in Amateur Soccer

In amateur soccer technique and tactical training receive too little attention – especially in the lower divisions. It is exactly here where responsible trainers should place more emphasis. This can be done with technique training of the "old school," or it can be made very interesting with special playing forms and tasks.

The typical characteristics of the game call for not only individual but also team specific technique and tactics training.

Control over the ball is extremely difficult for every player and the exactness of actions during the game suffers from imperfection in dealing with the medium "ball."

On the one hand the available space, the playing field, limits the player's spatial capacity for development with the ball, on the other hand the variety of technically and tactically possible actions is unlimited.

The distribution of the playing tasks therefore plays an important part in involving all players in the game. The team is thus positioned according to functional and positional aspects.

Three playing field positions – defense, midfield and forwards – can be found. Within such a group of positions the actors must carry out certain playing tasks.

The objective "score goals" and "prevent goals" is the focal point of the playing action and forces the individual players in their positions to develop certain techniques and tactics of "attack" or "defense."

Nevertheless the tactical training must not be restricted to the playing positions alone. It is much more important that the players have a technical ability which allows them to act – but also to react – variably and creatively.

Improvisation and creativity can be improved and refined through systematic technique training. This automatically leads to better exploitation of the tactical capacities of a player and the whole team.

The prescribed playing order, and with it the tactical concept, often constrain players in their positions so much that the attractiveness of the game suffers and it loses its "playful character."

In fact it is the risky and unplannable actions which make the game interesting and varied.

A too rigid limiting of the players to their playing positions would decidedly reduce the quality of the game, if not make it impossible. The dynamism of the game thrives on spontaneous actions, i.e. improvisation, and playing culture must be tried out and learnt in training.

Because of the complex game structure, in training the participant needs to be confronted again and again with situations that meet its demands. This is best achieved through game-like tasks that imitate the "big game."

In 2:2 or 4:4 games with small goals such elements are optimally available and trainable. Defense and attack behavior are trained and intensified in such a task situation.

The tactical task situation which is to be dealt with in competition must be practiced intensively during the week.

Experience shows, however, that in the lower amateur field with a maximum of two training sessions per week this is very difficult to accomplish.

Here in particular the above mentioned playing tasks must therefore be given special attention.

**Note:** The tactical concept is based first and foremost on the available players and not on the trainer's ideas.

### The tactical concept

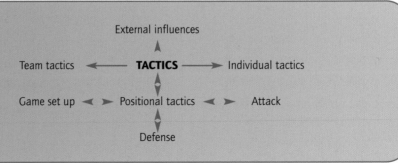

The general tactical attitude is binding for every player.
We differentiate:

### 1. Individual tactics

- Covering, break aways, goal shots, dribbling, passing, center passing.
- Heading, tackling, handing over, taking-over, shifting.

### 2. Team tactics

- Defensive tactics, offensive tactics, playing for time, countering tactics, pressing, game systems (4:3:3; 4:2:4; 3:5:2, etc.), forechecking.

  Forechecking means: As early as possible the opposing team is attacked in its own half in order to make it difficult for them to get their game together.

### 3. Positional tactics

- Attack: playing on the wing, playing through the forwards, defense measures, pressing, forechecking, shifting the game.
- Game set up: playing on the wing, diagonal, cross and through passes, keeping the ball, covering a space or a man.
- Defense: securing, offside trap, covering a space or a man, clearance, offensive play.

### 4. External influences

- Opponent's qualities: degree of fitness, technical skills, tactical skills, mental strengths.
- Conditions on day of play: weather, condition of field, size of field, home advantage, spectator behavior.
- Game situation: goal kick, kick-off, corner, free kick, penalty, throw in, interruption of play.
- State of play: trailing, leading, 1st or 2nd half, draw, team in majority or minority.
- League position: rising/championship chances, relegation, midfield.

# 6 Training Periods and Planning

By training periodization we mean the dividing of training into short sections (periods, cycles) which each have a different emphasis. Training periods arise because for biological reasons no player can always be in top form and because training structures and content must be periodically adapted to developments in sport. Thus the training plans for the preparatory, competition and transitional periods reflect the timing and content of the training effort in each case.

German amateur soccer assumes an average of 48 weeks per year (see Fig. 2). If a winter-break is taken the following schedule should be followed but could be tailored to shorter seasons.

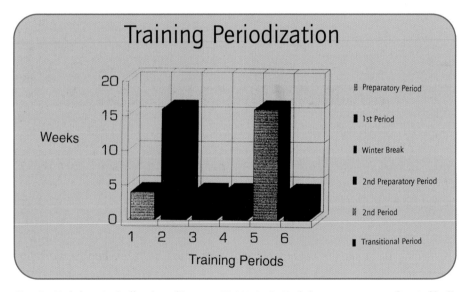

*Fig. 2: Training Periodization (Source: FRANK, G: Trainingsprogramme für Fußball-Amateurvereine, 4th ed. 1988)*

The training and competition year is divided as follows:
1st preparatory period (pre-season) 4-6 weeks; 1st competition period 16 weeks; 2nd preparatory period 4 weeks; 2nd competition period 16 weeks; transitional period 4-6 weeks.

The annual program of amateur soccer differs from country to country. German amateur soccer serves as an example, the described training and competition periods can be tailored individually.

The individual periods can be considered flexibly, according to the players' level. The annual training plan must exactly consider the distribution of amount and intensity (see Fig. 3).

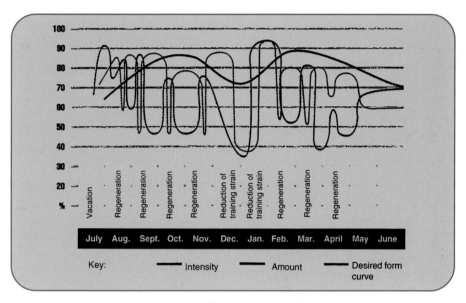

*Fig. 3: Training strain in annual cycle (The diagram was taken from issue 5 + 6/1995 of the magazine "fussballtraining." Reproduced with kind permission of Philippka-Verlag, Münster, Germany.)*

In training planning the various playing levels must be taken into consideration accordingly.

The lower levels usually train twice a week. From medium level up to elite level the number of training days increases to a maximum of four days, often with two training units per day.

The training programs are therefore devised in such a way that the coach can choose the training contents he needs and vary or supplement them depending on the level(s) he is working with.

The contents and objectives of the training programs are designed for adult teams and should not be simply transferred to children's and youth training without adjustment.

Content and training emphasis can vary from week to week depending on the playing strength of the team, always taking the last match played as a base mark. An extra goal keeper training has not been included as this is usually carried out within the team training. In the middle and higher levels goal keeper training should be done individually.

Correct periodization begins with the preparatory period, which we divide into two areas:
1. Preparatory period in general – with heavy strain in the amount of training and increasing intensity. Daily training is designed, especially in the top levels, to increase general physical fitness – endurance, strength, jumping ability and speed.

2. Preparatory period in particular areas – with intensive training of technique and game speed, development of feeling for the ball, teamwork and integrating new players into the team. The ball should always be the focal point of training. Training games complete the program.

Attention should be paid to weather conditions in early training – heat, humidity etc. Professional soccer would probably use Monday as a day of care and regeneration and then train on during the week with a team-meeting on Friday.

A training camp at the beginning of the pre-season training is generally only useful at the highest level.

Training in the lower levels would probably take place on Tuesday and Thursday and would be tailored to the forthcoming match i.e. they are designed to lead to intensification and improvement in physical form and refinement of technique, tactics and teamwork.

Training should reach its zenith in October/November. At this time it is sourced to establish so-called "strain reminders" regarding strength and endurance.

If a winter break takes place, a slight reduction in fitness has to be accepted and is then made good in the following (second) preparatory period.

In the second preparatory period the relationship of intensity and amount of training to one another is increased in order to raise the fitness level again.

During this time friendly matches serve to improve teamwork in the sectors defense, mid-field and forwards.

In late February/early March the second round begins. The training strain corresponds to that of the first competition period. The amount and intensity of this strain are determined by the strain and requirements of the championship round (relegation, championship).

The increasing strain of competition matches must be compensated for by a reduction of the amount of training.

The training content is directed towards maintaining general and specific fitness, achieved through competition exercises or special training.

Playing exercise forms and tasks provide for optimum physical and psychological recovery.

# 7   Organisational Tips

The training programs have been devised in such a way that fitness, technique and tactics are systematically improved.

Changes within the individual training units are possible and desirable, but the trainer should make sure that the fitness of his players matches competition demands (if necessary, individual training for injured or less fit players).

The trainer should have the following aids:

1.  Whistle
2.  Stopwatch
3.  Balls (in sufficient numbers – at least one ball/pair)
4.  Medicine balls
5.  Slalom poles with horizontal bars that can be converted into hurdles and goals
7.  Team jerseys
7.  Sufficient number of skipping ropes
8.  Weight vests for rehabilitation training
9.  Elastic bands for rehabilitation training
10. Red-white building tape for dividing up playing fields, etc.
11. Old folding up benches (beer garden benches) are extremely well suited for double pass and goal keeper training.

# 8   Performance Measurement

In amateur soccer objective performance measurement designed to describe the current physical condition of a player is usually only possible with great effort (e.g. measuring maximum ability to take in oxygen).

Therefore trainers in the amateur field must restrict themselves to more simple methods.

Measurement that is purely soccer related is only possible through playing performance, the interpretation of which is not without problems. Tests can only measure certain abilities such as endurance, strength, speed, etc.

The pulse (number of heartbeats per time unit of a healthy person) can serve as a criterion for the current capacity and training condition of an individual.

At rest the heart of a physically untrained person beats between 60-80 times/min. A person who does endurance training has a pulse at rest of between 30-50 beats/min. The better the training condition in connection with endurance training, the lower the resting pulse rate will be. Top rates of 220 beats/min under full strain are not rare.

Another criterion for judging the degree of physical fitness is the relationship between the working pulse  and the recovery pulse rates (measured two min after work finishes). The faster the pulse rate approaches the resting pulse value, the better the general physical condition.

The most accurate method of measurement is the ECG (electrocardiogram) on a running or cycling machine. As amateur clubs will seldom have access to such devices, the pulse rate can be measured with a pulse measuring device (ear clip, finger clip). Modern devices with a chest belt can also be used. Measuring by hand, however, only provides very inexact information.

A very popular test is the so-called COOPER-TEST (endurance test), named after KENNETH COOPER. This test only measures the stamina of the players and gives no information on other abilities.
   On a well measured circuit (400 m track), as great a distance as possible should be covered in twelve minutes.

### Evaluation

| Fitness (stamina) | up to 30 years | 30-40 years |
| --- | --- | --- |
| Very good | 3,000 m and more | 2,850 m |
| Good | 2,600 m | 2,450 m |
| Satisfactory | 2,400 m | 2,250 m |
| Insufficient | 2,000 m | 1,900 m |

# 9 **Explanation of Symbols**

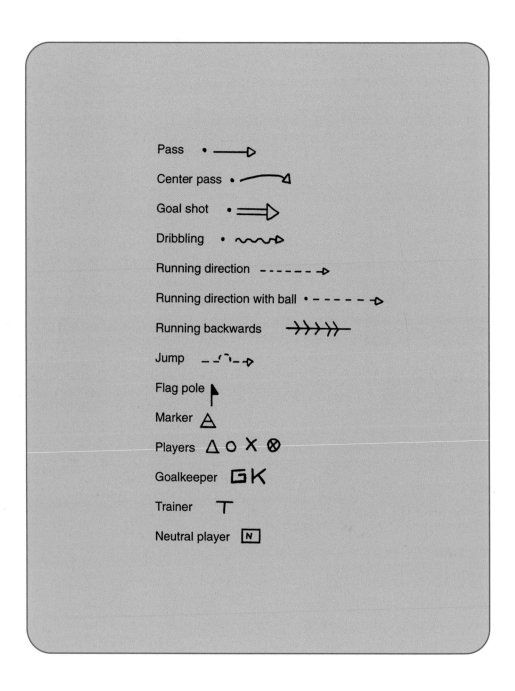

Pass

Center pass

Goal shot

Dribbling

Running direction

Running direction with ball

Running backwards

Jump

Flag pole

Marker

Players

Goalkeeper

Trainer

Neutral player

# 10 Training Programs

The training programs are designed in such a way that the contents and training emphasis can be adapted according to the playing level. The following classifications allow a coach to decide what level his team slots into: elite level, top level, medium level, lower levels (top lower level, standard lower level).

Each trainer must select the training features most suited to his and his team's needs and adapt these to the weekly game and competition schedule. The time dedicated to the individual training elements should be decided on flexibly.

For the warm-up and cool-down exact times are not always given. This is left up to the trainers. The warm-up can of course be carried out with a ball.

The programs are numbered. Two training units per week have been prepared for a 48 week year. Additional or modified training units must be created by trainers to suit their needs e.g. for a shorter season.

# Program 1

**1st Preparational Period**
**1st Week**

| TRAINING FEATURE | ORGANISATION/AMOUNT/TIPS |
|---|---|
| **Warm-up:**<br>Jogging | • Preparation for the forest run<br>• Welcome players at beginning of season<br>• 5 min |
| **Fitness:**<br>Basic endurance | • Forest or cross-country run<br>• 5 km-run in such a way that a pulse of 150/min is reached<br>• After the run 5 min walking and stretching |
| **Technique:**<br>Individual techniques<br><br><br><br>Goal shot<br> | • Running with the ball/juggling the ball<br>• Shadow dribbling – one partner runs ahead with the ball, the other must imitate every movement<br>• One ball/player<br><br>• Keep the ball up in a group of 4<br>• Play 5:2 in marked field<br>• 15-20 min<br><br><br>• In penalty area |

- From kick-off circle

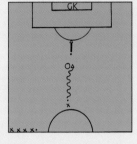

- From playoff 1:1
- 15-20 min

**Tactics:**

Running around freely –
game without ball

- Game 5:5
- 5 x 2 min – stretching after each series

Closing game

- Game 11:11
- Game 8:8 (elite/top level)
- 20 min

**Cool-down:**

Slowly running around

- 5 min

# Program 2

**1st Preparational Period**
**1st Week**

| TRAINING FEATURE | ORGANISATION/AMOUNT/TIPS |
|---|---|
| **Warm-up:**<br>Jogging | • Preparation for forest run |
| **Fitness:**<br>Basic endurance | • Forest or cross-country run<br>• 6 km – 150 pulse/min<br>• 2x/wk (medium level and above)<br>• After the run, stretching |
| **Technique:**<br>Individual technique | • Game 5:5 with the "weaker foot" only<br>• Two ball contacts/player (top/elite level)<br>• 15 min |
| Goal shot | • By center pass from right and left |
| | • After slalom dribble from kick-off circle<br>• 20 min<br>• 2 x/wk (top/elite level) |
| Variation: | • With defense player |

**Tactics:**

Break away

- Game without ball – game 5:5
- Task: After passing, immediately break away
- 3 x 5 min with short breaks
- Two ball contacts/player (medium level and above)

Closing game

- Game 11:11 (Bachelors – Husbands)
- Game 6:6 (medium level and above)
- 20 min

**Cool-down:**

Loosening up exercises

- See stretching exercises

# Program 3

**1st Preparational Period
2nd Week**

| TRAINING FEATURE | ORGANISATION/AMOUNT/TIPS |
|---|---|
| **Warm-up:**<br>Jogging | • Preparation for forest run |
| **Fitness:**<br>Basic endurance | • Forest or cross country run<br>• 6 km – 150 pulse/min<br>• 2 x/week (wk) (top/elite level)<br>• After the run, stretching |
| **Technique:**<br>Individual technique | • Each player practices alone.<br>• One ball/player<br>• 15 min |
| **Goal shot** | • From playoff 1:1 |
| | • After kick from kick-off circle |

| | |
|---|---|
| **Variation:** | • With opponent (medium level and above)<br>• 15 min<br>• 2x/wk (medium level and above) |

**Tactics:**

Counter play
- Game 5:5 with small goals
- Task: After possession of the ball quick change to offensive – through forward pass
- 2x/wk (medium level and above)
- 20 min

Closing game
- Game 11:11
- Game 8:6 (medium level and above) Majority vs. minority on 3/4 of field

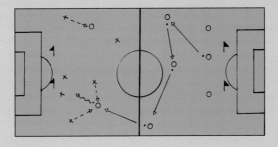

**Cool-down:**

Slowly running around
- Stretching

# Program 4

**1st Preparational Period**
**2nd Week**

| TRAINING FEATURE | ORGANISATION/AMOUNT/TIPS |
|---|---|
| **Warm-up:**<br>Jogging | • Preparation for forest run |
| **Fitness:**<br>Basic endurance | • Forest or cross-country run<br>• 6 km – 160 pulse/min<br>• 2 x/wk (medium level and above)<br>• After the run, stretching |
| Speed | • 20 m sprints<br>• 15 sprints – after each sprint 30 s break with loosening up exercises |
| Variation: | • With about turn<br>• 2x/wk (medium level and above) |
| **Technique:**<br>Header | • Header in groups of 4<br>• In a circle<br><br>• Zigzag |

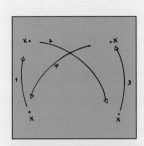

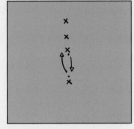

- In a row

- 15 min

**Goal shot**

- Practicing freely
- 15 min
- 2x/wk (medium level and above)

**Tactics:**
Game without ball

- Game 7:7 on half the field
- 3 x 5 min – after each series a short break
- Two ball contacts/player (top/elite level)

Closing game

- Game 11:11
- Game 5:5
- 20 min
- 2x/wk (medium level and above)

**Cool-down:**
Slowly running around

# Program 5

**1st Preparational Period**
**3rd Week**

| TRAINING FEATURE | ORGANISATION/AMOUNT/TIPS |
|---|---|
| **Warm-up:**<br>Jogging | • Preparation for forest run |
| **Fitness:**<br>Basic endurance | • Forest or cross-country run<br>• 7 km − 160 pulse/min<br>• 2 x/wk (medium level and above)<br>• After the run, stretching |
| **Technique:**<br>Individual technique<br><br> | • Game with the "weak foot"<br>• Game 4:4 with small goals − goals can be shot from in front and behind<br>• 2x/wk (medium level and above)<br>• 3 x 5 min − short break after each series |
| Goal shot | • Practicing freely<br>• From playoff 2:2 starting at the center line<br>• 2x/wk (medium level and above)<br>• 20 min |

**Tactics:**
Playing together and covering the field

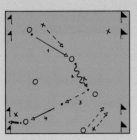

- Game 6:6 with small goals – each team can assault two goals and must defend two goals

**Variation:**

- Two ball contacts/player (medium level and above)
- 2x/wk (top/elite level)

Closing game

- Game 11:11
- 20 min

**Cool-down:**
Slowly running around

# Program 6

**1st Preparational Period**
**3rd Week**

| TRAINING FEATURE | ORGANISATION/AMOUNT/TIPS |
|---|---|
| **Warm-up:**<br>Jogging | • Preparation for forest run |
| **Fitness:**<br>Endurance test | • 12 min endurance test (COOPER-TEST)<br>• Test area: 400 m track<br>• Start in groups<br>• Evaluation, see Chapter 7, Performance Measurement |
| Speed | • 15 m sprints<br>• 15 sprints – after each sprint 30 s break with loosening up exercises<br>• 2x/wk (medium level and above) |
| **Technique:**<br>Header | • Three players circle another, who throws the ball up, and head it back to him while jumping<br>• After several rounds, change roles<br>• 10 min |

**Goal shot**

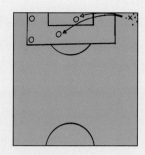

Center pass from corner flag
- 3-4 players are in the penalty area
- Center pass after 1:1 from corner flag
- 2x/wk (medium level and above)
- In groups
- 20 min

**Tactics:**

One on one behavior

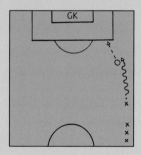

- Game 1:1 – the pairs practice along the sideline. The defender turns his outer side towards the attacker
- 20 min
- 2x/wk (medium level and above)

Closing game

- Game 11:11
- Two ball contacts/player (top/elite level)
- 25 min

**Cool-down:**

Slowly running around

- Barefoot, if grass field available

# Program 7

**1st Preparational Period
4th Week**

| TRAINING FEATURE | ORGANISATION/AMOUNT/TIPS |
| --- | --- |
| **Warm-up:**<br>Jogging | • Preparation for forest run |
| **Fitness:**<br>Basic endurance | • Forest or cross-country run<br>• 7 km – 160 pulse/min<br>• After the run, stretching<br>• 2x/wk (medium level and above) |
| **Technique:**<br>Individual technique | • Each player practices his own particular techniques, feints and tricks<br>• 2x/wk (medium level and above)<br>• 15 min |
| Goal shot | • Outplaying the goalkeeper – start with the ball from the center line<br>• Practice in groups<br>• 2x/wk (medium level and above)<br>• 15 min |
| **Tactics:**<br>Quick escape from covering player | • An extra player and a pair of players stand about 20 m apart. The covered player must try to get away from his coverer using a feint and pass the ball to the extra player.<br>• 20 min |

| Variation: | • Extra player has two pairs to whom he alternately passes the ball |
| Closing game | • Game majority vs. minority<br>11:8 – Task: The minority team tries to keep the ball in its "own ranks" for as long as possible<br>• 20 min<br>• Game 7:5 across field width |

**Cool-down:**
Stretching

# Program 8

**1st Preparational Period**
**4th Week**

| TRAINING FEATURE | ORGANISATION/AMOUNT/TIPS |
| --- | --- |
| **Warm-up:**<br>Jogging and stretching<br>Game 5:2 in a square | • 10 min<br>• 10 min (medium level and above) |
| **Fitness:**<br>Speed<br><br><br><br>Variation: | • 20 m sprints<br>• 15 x<br>• After each sprint 30 s break<br>• 2x/wk (medium level and above)<br>• Pairs alternate, each partner runs and gives hand signal to partner at 20 m line |
| **Technique:**<br>Individual technique | • Game 5:5 with small goals, play is only allowed with the "weak foot," otherwise possession is changed<br>• 15 min |

| | |
|---|---|
| Goal shot | • Practicing freely<br>• Only lower and middle playing levels<br>• 20 min |
| **Tactics:**<br>Countering in defense<br><br><br><br><br>**Variation:** | • Game 6:6 – Task: After possession immediately switch to countering<br>• Suitable means: through balls<br>• 2x/wk (medium level and above)<br>• 15 min<br>• Game 11:11 – Task: For the midfield players, after possession immediately switch to countering (through balls to both wings)<br>• 35 min |
| **Cool-down:**<br>Slowly running around and stretching | |

# Program 9

**1st Preparational Period**
**5th Week**

| TRAINING FEATURE | ORGANISATION/AMOUNT/TIPS |
|---|---|
| **Warm-up:**<br>Game 5:2 | • Two ball contacts/player<br>• 15 min |
| **Technique:**<br>Juggling the ball<br><br>Header duel | • Groups of three<br>• Ball must be kept in the air<br><br>• Two players stand close together and try to head back the ball when it is thrown |

- As above
- Lined up in a row, back person heads back the ball
- Role change on trainer's command
- 20 min

**Goal shot**

- Practicing freely – in groups
- With center passes from right and left
- 15 min

**Fitness:**
Endurance specific to soccer

- Game 8:8 across long side of field
- Task: After ball has been lost into opponent's half, immediately run into own half
- Short break after 10 min with loosening up and stretching exercises
- 2x/wk (medium level and above)
- 20 min

**Variation:**

- Practicing can be carried out as a competition

**Tactics:**
Understanding of the game

- Game 5:5 – three predetermined defense players may only touch the ball twice each; the two forwards can dribble.
- 2x/wk (medium level and above)
- 20 min

**Variation:**

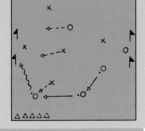

- Game 11:11 with the same task for the defense players
- 25 min

**Variation:**

- Game 5:5:5 – one team always has a break
- 3 x 8 min

**Cool-down:**
Slowly running around

# Program 10

**1st Preparational Period**
**5th Week**

| TRAINING FEATURE | ORGANISATION/AMOUNT/TIPS |
|---|---|
| **Warm-up:**<br>Game 5:2 | • 10 min |
| Jogging and stretching | • 10 min |
| **Fitness:**<br>Circuit training<br>(Ability to jump and speed endurance) | • Station 1<br>• Move ball at max. speed and change directions |
| | • Station 2<br>• Game 1:1 or 2:2 |
| | • Station 3<br>• Throw ball for header, standing<br>• One partner throws, the other heads back, jumping |
| | • Station 4<br>• 10 m sprints with about turn |
| Strain: 60 s/station, then role swap | |
| Break: 60 s/station | |
| Series: 5 x | • 2x/wk (top/elite level) |
| Break in series: 3 min | • Stretching<br>• ca. 20 min |

## Technique:
Goal shot

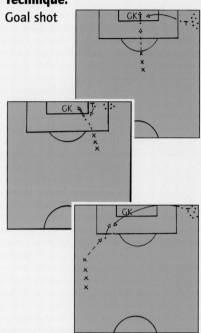

- Trainer throws balls, which must be headed into the goal

- Trainer throws the balls from the front
- Start from edge of penalty area

- Trainer throws high flying balls into the penalty area which must immediately be shot
- Practice in groups
- 20 min

## Tactics:
Covering the field

- Game 6:6
- Task: After losing the ball in the opponent's half, immediately run back to the allotted half
- 2x/wk (medium level and above)
- 20 min

Closing game

- 11:11
- Task: Use the tactic just practiced

Variation:

- Game 5:5:5
- One team takes a break and jogs around the field
- 20 min

## Cool-down:
Loosening up exercises

# Program 11

**1st Preparational Period**
**6th Week**

| TRAINING FEATURE | ORGANISATION/AMOUNT/TIPS |
|---|---|
| **Warm-up:**<br>Relaxed trot / stretching | • 5-7 min |
| **Technique:**<br>Individual technique<br>Game with the "weak foot" | • Game 4:4 with small goals<br><br>• The ball can only be kicked with the "weak foot"<br>• 2x/wk (medium level and above)<br>• Two ball contacts (top lower level and above)<br>• Goals can be shot from in front and behind<br>• 15 min |
| Goal shot<br> | • After a double pass with trainer or other player |
| | • After dribbling 1:1 from the center line |

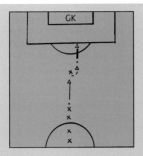

- After kick-off – kicker stands with back to goal

**Variation:**

- With opponent
- 2x/wk (top lower level and above)
- Practice in groups
- 20-25 min

**Fitness:**
Endurance specific to football

- Game 8:8 with small goals – half field
- Two ball contacts/player (medium level and above)
- 25 min

**Tactics:**
Changing position during offensive

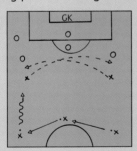

- Game 5:5 starting at center line
- Both forwards swap positions with ball in front of opposing defense
- Textbook practice
- 2x/wk (top level and above)
- 20-25 min

Closing game

- Game 11:11
- Lower levels only
- 25-30 min

**Cool-down:**
Slowly running around

# Program 12

**1st Preparational Period**
**6th Week**

| TRAINING FEATURE | ORGANISATION/AMOUNT/TIPS |
|---|---|
| **Warm-up:**<br>Jogging and stretching | • In groups<br>• 7-10 min |
| Game 5:2 | • Top lower level and above<br>• 10 min |
| **Technique:**<br>Individual technique | • Each player practices alone or in groups<br>• One ball/player<br>• 15 min |
| **Tactics:**<br>Countering<br> | • Game 6:6 with the task: Get the two forwards into the game with diagonal passes<br>• Textbook practice starting at the center line<br>• 2x/wk (medium level and above)<br>• 20-25 min |
| **Fitness:**<br>Speed endurance | • Intensification runs<br>• 6 x 3 runs down the entire field length<br>• After each series 3 min break<br>• 2x/wk (top/elite level) |
| Closing game | • Game 11:11 with task: Countering with diagonal passes<br>• 25 min |
| **Cool-down:**<br>Slowly running around | |

# Program 13

**1st Competition Period**
**1st Week**

| TRAINING FEATURE | ORGANISATION/AMOUNT/TIPS |
|---|---|
| **Warm-up:**<br>Game 5:2 | • 10 min. |
| **Technique:**<br>Short passing game | • In a circle<br>• Four players run in a circle and pass the ball to each other while running. |
| | • Lined up<br>• The players stand in a line and one passes to the first in the line. After returning the pass he goes to the back of the line. |
| **Variation:** | • After returning the pass the player runs to the passer and stands behind him. |
| **Goal shot** | • Parallel<br>• Four players run parallel from one side of the field to the other, passing the ball backwards and forwards.<br>• 20-25 min<br>• Practicing freely<br>• In groups<br>• 20 min |

**Fitness:**

Endurance specific to soccer

- Game 5:5 + goalkeeper on half the field

- 2 x/wk (medium level and above)
- 20 min

Closing game

- Game 8:8 + two goalkeepers with the task: Midfield players are allowed two ball contacts/player.
- 30 min

**Cool-down:**

Slowly running around/stretching

# Program 14

**1st Competition Period**
**1st Week**

| TRAINING FEATURE | ORGANISATION/AMOUNT/TIPS |
|---|---|
| **Warm-up:**<br>Jogging and stretching | • 15 min |
| **Technique:**<br>Short passing game<br>"Play and go"<br>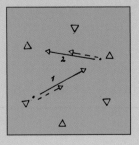 | • Six players stand in a circle, each player follows his ball to the position passed to, etc.<br>• 2 x/wk (top lower level and above) |

| Game 3:1 | • Three players stand in a circle and pass the ball to each other, the fourth has to struggle for possession (with role swap)<br>• 20 min |

**Fitness:**
Speed

- 20 m sprints – 15x
- 30 s break between sprints
- 2 x/wk (medium level and above)

**Variation:**

- Beginning from crouching position
- Beginning lying on stomach
- Beginning lying on back
- Beginning standing on one leg
- Beginning from a skip

**Tactics:**
Covering
the field

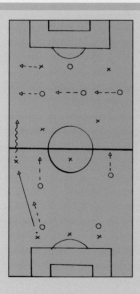

- Game 8:10 with the task:
- Midfield players, on losing the ball in the opponents' half, must quickly "sink and move in the direction of the ball"
- Methodically practice
- Only medium level and above
- 2 x/wk (medium level and above)
- 25 min

**Variation:**

- Analyse mistakes in championship game and eradicate them through specific practice

Closing game

- Game 11:11
- 25 min

**Cool-down:**
Slowly running around

- Barefoot, if on grass field

# Program 15

**1st Competition Period
2nd Week**

| TRAINING FEATURE | ORGANISATION/AMOUNT/TIPS |
|---|---|
| **Warm-up:**<br>Trotting/stretching | • 10 min |
| Game 5:2 | • Medium level and above<br>• Two ball contacts/player<br>• Direct play<br>• 10 min |
| **Technique:**<br>Goal shot<br> | • After corners from right and left |
| | • After double pass from center line<br><br><br>• 2 x/wk (medium level and above)<br>• Practice in groups<br>• 20-25 min |
| **Fitness:**<br>Strength, strength at speed, | • "Scuffle ball" with a medicine ball on<br>strength endurance, reactions<br>a 40 x 20 m field |

| | |
|---|---|
| | • Goals are only allowed when all players of the team in ball possession are in the opponents' half. |
| | • 20 min |
| Duel for the ball | • Game 2:2:2 with small goals |
| | • One team always takes a break |
| | • Playing time 5 min |
| | • Two sessions everyone vs. everyone |
| | • 30 min |

**Tactics:**
Closing game

• Game 11:11 free play
• 20 min

**Cool-down:**
Slowly running around/stretching

# Program 16

**1st Competition Period**
**2nd Week**

| TRAINING FEATURE | ORGANISATION/AMOUNT/TIPS |
|---|---|
| **Warm-up:**<br>Game 4:2 | • Group of four – two ball contacts/player<br>• Group of two can dribble<br>• 10 min |
| **Technique:**<br>Corners  | • Have the ball played with side to and from the goal<br>• Practice in groups |

High distance passes

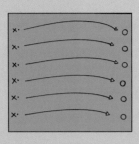

- Standing
- Moving
- Stopping with the chest
- 25-30 min

## Tactics:
Getting behind the defense

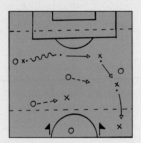

- Game 5:5 on half field
- A 5 m wide corridor between center line and goal out line may only be entered by one player from the attacking team at a time, who must get behind the opposing defenders.

- 2 x/wk (top/elite level)
- Not for lower levels
- 25 min

**Variation:**

- Game 5:5:5 with small goals
- Half field
- One team always has a break and jogs around the field.
- Task: Quick change from attack to defense
- 10 min/game

Closing game

- 11:11
- 25-30 min

## Cool-down:
Loosening exercises

# Program 17

**1st Competition Period**
**3rd Week**

| TRAINING FEATURE | ORGANISATION/AMOUNT/TIPS |
|---|---|
| **Warm-up:** | |
| Jogging/stretching | • 10 min |
| | |
| Game 5:2 | • 15 min |
| **Fitness:** | |
| Speed | • 20 m sprints |
| | • 2 x 10 m sprints |
| | • 30 s break between sprints |
| | • 15 min break between series |
| | • Light ball play (active recovery) |
| | |
| Endurance specific to soccer | • Game 7:7 on half field |
| | • Two ball contacts/player |
| | • 2 x/wk (medium level and above) |
| | • 35 min – with short breaks |
| **Tactics:** | |
| Understanding of the game | • Game 7:7 on 3/4 of field |
| | • Task: Forcing a double pass |
| | • 2 x/wk (medium level and above) |
| Variation: | • Reduction to 2/3 of field |
| | • 25 min |

| | |
|---|---|
| Closing game | • Game 11:11<br>• 1st team against reserves<br>• 25 min |

**Cool-down:**
Jogging and loosening exercises

# Program 18

**1st Competition Period**
**3rd Week**

| TRAINING FEATURE | ORGANISATION/AMOUNT/TIPS |
|---|---|
| **Warm-up:**<br>Throw in game<br>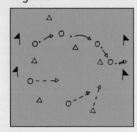<br>Game 5:2 | • The ball can only be played on after a correct throw in. Goals can be scored with feet and head.<br>• Six players/team<br>• Field 40 x 20 m<br>• 15 min<br><br>• 15 min |
| **Fitness:**<br>Speed with the ball | • 20 m sprints with the ball<br>• 15 x – 30 s break between sprints (active ball play) |
| **Technique:**<br>Goal shot | • Free practice<br>• In groups<br>• 2 x/wk (top lower level and above)<br>• 20 min |

**Tactics:**

Countering

- Game 5:5 on half field with small goals. In one's own half the ball may only pass between a maximum of three positions in order to get quickly into the opponents' half.
- If the ball goes to more than three positions, it must be given to the opponents.
- 25 min

**Variation:**

- Determine in advance the players who may be the three positions played to.

Closing game

- Game 7:7:7 on 3/4 field
- One team takes a break.
- 25 min

**Cool-down:**

Slowly running around/stretching

# Program 19

**1st Competition Period**
**4th Week**

| TRAINING FEATURE | ORGANISATION/AMOUNT/TIPS |
|---|---|
| **Warm-up:** Game 3:3 | • 15 min |
| **Technique:** Individual techniques | • Each player improves his personal strengths with the ball, e.g. dribbling, juggling with both feet, slalom running, heading etc. |

- Trainer gives tips.
- Include short breaks with stretching
- 20 min

**Fitness:**
Speed

- Sprints with the ball and abrupt turn
- 2 x 10 sprints
- 30 s break between sprints

**Tactics:**
Duel for the ball

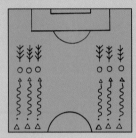

- Game 1:1 (defense player vs. forward)
- Trainer gives tips.
- Opposite ball and opponent, eye contact with team-mates
- Game 2:1 (two forwards vs. one defender)
- From the center line towards goal

**Variation:**

- Close with goal shot
- 2 x/wk (medium level and above)
- 20 min

Closing game

- Game 11:11
- Game 7:7 (two ball contacts/game; direct play; free play)

**Cool-down:**
Slowly running around/ loosening exercises

# Program 20

**1st Competition Period**
**4th Week**

| TRAINING FEATURE | ORGANISATION/AMOUNT/TIPS |
|---|---|
| **Warm-up:**<br>Jogging and stretching | • 15 min |
| **Fitness:**<br>Speed | • 25 sprints<br>• 15 x<br>• 30 s break between sprints<br>• 2 x/wk (medium level and above) |
| **Technique:**<br>Goal shot | • After sprint from the goal out line behind the penalty area<br><br>• After heading duel starting at center line<br><br>• After double pass with trainer and against a defender |

- From game 2:2 starting at center line

- 25 min

## Tactics:
Playing for goal opportunities

- Game 4:4 from center line
- Four players line up behind the center line and begin an attack on the goal. The attack is over when either a goal is scored, the defense has the ball or the ball is out. Then the four line up behind the center line again.
- 2 x/wk (medium level and above)
- 25-30 min

Closing game

- Game 11:11
- Task: The team in possession of the ball is only allowed two ball contacts/player within the opponents' half.
- Fast goal shooting
- 20 min

## Cool-down:
Slowly running around/loosening exercises

# Program 21

**1st Competition Period**
**5th Week**

| TRAINING FEATURE | ORGANISATION/AMOUNT/TIPS |
|---|---|
| **Warm-up:**<br>Moving with the ball in penalty area<br>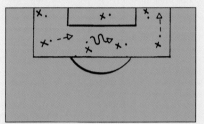 | • All players are in the penalty area with a ball and run amongst each other.<br>• Trainer calls changes of directions.<br>• Forwards, backwards, sideways, reverse<br>• With speed change – slow, medium, fast<br>• With feints |
| **Variation:** | • All players move to the other penalty area<br>• 15 min<br>• Finish with stretching |
| **Technique:**<br>Dribbling and feints | • Two partners practice all the feints they know<br>• With role swap<br>• As above – but with small goals<br>• 2 x/wk (top lower level and above)<br>• 20 min |
| **Fitness:**<br>Endurance specific to soccer | • Game 6:6 on half field<br>• Two ball contacts/player<br>• direct play<br>• 2 x/wk (medium level and above)<br>• 30 min |

**Tactics:**
Playing for goal opportunities

- Game 4:4 + 1

- On the edge of the penalty area the playing field is divided off into a goal zone in which there is a player from the attacking team.
  The attacking team has to wait, by skilfully keeping the ball, until this player has freed himself from the opposing defense. Only he may shoot goals.
  After a successful goal the game re-commences at the center line.

- Back passes from the goal zone are allowed.
- 2 x/wk (medium level and above)
- 25 min

**Cool-down:**
Slowly running around

# Program 22

**1st Competition Period**
**5th Week**

| TRAINING FEATURE | ORGANISATION/AMOUNT/TIPS |
|---|---|
| **Warm-up:**<br>Jogging/stretching | • 15 min |
| **Technique:**<br>Individual techniques | • Two partners practice together.<br>• Keep the ball up both standing and moving around<br>• Fast flat passing over 10 m<br>• Standing/moving<br>• Stopping with the chest/thigh/foot after a high pass<br>• Standing and moving<br>• Dribbling – methodically<br>• Shadow dribbling by the partner<br>• Feinting during fast run with the ball (stopping, about turn etc.)<br>• Swap partners within the practice groups<br><br>• 15-20 min |
| **Goal shot** | • After kick-off at chest height in penalty area (position with back to goal) |

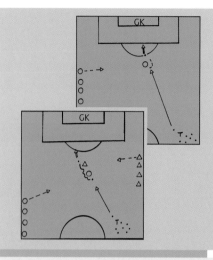

- After flat kick-off near penalty area (as above)

- Practicing as above
- With opponent
- 2 x/wk (medium level and above)
- 15-20 min

## Fitness:
Endurance specific to soccer

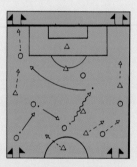

- Game 7:7 with two corner goals each which are set up on the goal out line and the center line.
- Both teams must defend both their goals.
- 2 x/wk (medium level and above)
- Two ball contacts/player (medium level and above)
- 3 x 10 min with short breaks

## Tactics:
Keeping the ball, slowing the pace

- Game 11:11
- Delay the ball with steady cross and back passes in own half, and then suddenly increase the pace with a fast double pass.

## Variation:

- Lower levels
- Free play
- 25-30 min

## Cool-down:
Slowly running around/loosening exercises

# Program 23

**1st Competition Period**
**6th Week**

| TRAINING FEATURE | ORGANISATION/AMOUNT/TIPS |
|---|---|
| **Warm-up:**<br>Ball across the line<br><br> | • Game 5:5 or 7:7 on half field<br>• Goal only counts if the ball is taken across one of the sidelines<br>• 15 min |
| Variation 5:2 | • Top/elite level<br>• Two ball contacts/player<br>• Direct play<br>• 15 min |
| **Fitness:**<br>Speed | • 30 m sprints<br>• 15 x – 30 s break between sprints<br>• 2 x/wk (top lower level and above)<br>• Stretching |
| **Technique:**<br>Individual techniques | • Flat pass, half high and high pass<br>• 20 m distance, 30 m distance; 40 m and more<br>• Center passes from full play from right and left<br>• Practice in groups<br>• 20 min |

**Tactics:**

Playing for goal opportunities

- Game 11:11
- Task: The team in possession must try to score a goal within a minute
- Otherwise ball goes to opponents
- 2 x/wk (medium level and above)

**Cool-down:**

Slowly running around/stretching

# Program 24

**1st Competition Period**
**6th Week**

| TRAINING FEATURE | ORGANISATION/AMOUNT/TIPS |
|---|---|
| **Warm-up:** | • Each player imitates the trainer's Playing the ball with eye contact to trainer running, stopping and about turn movements with the ball<br>• In penalty area<br>• In center circle<br>• Change from a penalty area to the other<br>• 15 min with short breaks<br>• Stretching |
| Game 5:2 | • Two ball contacts/player<br>• Direct play<br>• 10 min<br>• Stretching |
| **Technique:**<br>Dribbling, feints and using the ball doing station training | **Station 1**<br>• Game 2:2:2 on a field 25 x 20 m<br>• Team C plays towards Team A's goal. |

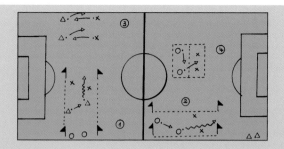

On scoring a goal or losing the ball, C plays against B, etc.

### Station 2
- Game 2:2:2 on a field 15 x 30 m with two goals per side
- One team always has a break.
- Only play with the "weak" foot.

### Station 3
- Heading in groups of two

### Station 4
- Football tennis on a 10 x 15 m field
- Three ball contacts in one's own half allowed
- Change of station after 5 min
- Two rounds (medium level and above)
- ca. 25 min

---

**Fitness:**
Endurance specific to soccer

- Game 7:7 on half field
- Two ball contacts/player
- Direct play (medium level and above)
- 30 min with short breaks/ stretching

---

**Cool-down:**
Slowly running around

# Program 25

**1st Competition Period**
**7th Week**

| TRAINING FEATURE | ORGANISATION/AMOUNT/TIPS |
|---|---|
| **Warm-up:**<br>Handball game | • Played to handball rules on a 40 x 20 m field with goals<br>• 15-20 min |
| Game 5:2 | • Two ball contacts<br>• Direct play<br>• 15 min |
| **Fitness:**<br>Speed | • 30 m sprints<br>• 15 x<br>• 30 s break between sprints<br>• 2 x/wk (medium level and above)<br>• Stretching |
| **Technique:**<br>Goal shot<br> | • After zigzag pass and center pass<br>• Two player pairs start from the center line, first right of it and then left of it, in the direction of the goal out line. The outer player plays a center pass or back pass to his partner, who then takes a goal shot.<br>• With opponent<br>• 25 min |
| Center passing from right and left | • From a stillstand<br>• From a run<br>• After slalom dribbling<br>• Medium level and above |

## Tactics:

Building up the game from the defensive
- Game 8:8 – Task: The defenders, when they get the ball, play to the two outer midfield players (midfield players stand ready along the sideline between center line and penalty area edge).
- 2 x/wk (medium level and higher)
- Defenders allowed only two ball contacts/ player
- 20 min

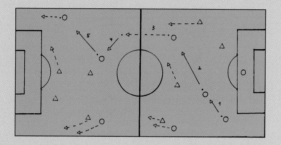

## Variation:

- Game 11:11
- Free play (lower levels)
- 25 min

## Cool-down:

Slowly running around

# Program 26

**1st Competition Period**
**7th Week**

| TRAINING FEATURE | ORGANISATION/AMOUNT/TIPS |
|---|---|
| **Warm-up:**<br>Game 3:1 | • 15 min – with role swap |
| Game 5:2 | • Two ball contacts/player<br>• Direct play<br>• Stretching<br>• 15 min |
| **Fitness:**<br>Speed with the ball | • Acceleration with the ball from ball control situation (on trainer's command)<br>• 3 x 10 accelerations over 10 m<br>• 3-5 min break between series<br>• 2 x/wk (medium level and above) |
| Endurance specific to soccer | • Game 8:8 on half field<br>• Two ball contacts/player<br>• Direct play (top/elite level)<br>• 20 min with short breaks |
| **Tactics:**<br>Wing play | • Game 4:4 on marked field |

| | |
|---|---|
| | • Two forwards hover near the center line and wait to receive the ball from their midfield players. After getting the ball one of them tries to dash to the goal. In the rectangle the game is continued with a new ball.<br>• Medium level and above<br>• 25 min |
| Closing game | • Game 11:11<br>• Team plays in formation for next championship game.<br>• 30 min |

**Cool-down:**
Slowly running around

# Program 27

**1st Competition Period**
**8th Week**

| TRAINING FEATURE | ORGANISATION/AMOUNT/TIPS |
|---|---|
| **Warm-up:**<br>Running and jumping | • Running, hopping gait, sideways gallop, jumps with half turn, crossing front and rear, running jumps, walking jumps, etc.<br>• Stretching<br>• 15 min |
| Game 5:2 | • 15 min |
| **Fitness:**<br>Speed | • 25 m sprints<br>• 2 x 10 sprints<br>• 30 s break between sprints |

- Break between series of 3-5 min active recovery (ball)
- 2 x/wk (medium level and above)
- Stretching

## Technique:
Free kick

- Free kicks in various forms
- Direct
- Indirect – after brief kick from fellow player
- One player plays across, the next stops with his foot, the third shoots.

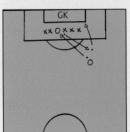

- After kick-off and bounce off player in the wall

- Practice in groups
- 2 x/wk (top/elite level)
- 25 min

## Tactics:
Teamwork and game overview

- Game 8:8 (three defense + five set up players) vs. reserves
- Task: No bad passes, confident teamwork
- Two ball contacts/player
- Direct play (top/elite level)
- 20 min

## Cool-down:
Loosening exercises

# Program 28

**1st Competition Period**
**8th Week**

| TRAINING FEATURE | ORGANISATION/AMOUNT/TIPS |
| --- | --- |
| **Warm-up:**<br>Jogging and stretching<br>Game 5:2 | • 25 min – 150 pulse/min<br>• Two ball contacts/player<br>• Direct play<br>• 25 min |
| **Fitness:**<br>Speed | • 15 m sprints with about turn<br>• 3 x 5 sprints<br>• 30 s break between sprints<br>• 5 min break between series<br>• 2 x/wk (medium level and above)<br>• Stretching |
| **Tactics:**<br>Pressing | • Game 6:6 on half field<br>• Task: On losing the ball in the opponent's half, all players move forward, immediately attack the player with the ball and cover the other opposing players. Because of the aggressive man against man tactics the opponent has difficulty getting his game together.<br>• 2 x/wk (medium level and above)<br>• 20 min |
| Closing game | • Game 11:11<br>• In own half two ball contacts/player, in the opponent's half free play<br>• 25 min |
| **Cool-down:**<br>Slowly running around | |

# Program 29

**1st Competition Period**
**9th Week**

| TRAINING FEATURE | ORGANISATION/AMOUNT/TIPS |
|---|---|
| **Warm-up:**<br>Running and working with the ball | • Each player runs with a ball and changes pace, direction and the way he controls the ball (according to trainer's instructions)<br>• Stretching<br>• 15 min |
| **Technique:**<br>Dribbling<br><br> | • One player dribbles towards another and tries to cross the sideline with the ball. |
| | • Dribbling while gaining ground, from the center line towards the goal |

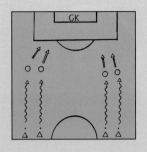

- Exercise as above
- With goal shot (defense player attacks determinedly)
- Change of partners
- 2 x/wk (medium level and above)
- 20 min

**Fitness:**
Playing speed

- Game 6:6 on half field
- Two ball contacts/player
- 5 x 3 min
- Go for maximum pace
- 5 min break between series
- 2 x/wk (top/elite level)
- ca. 35 min

**Cool-down:**
Slowly running around

# Program 30

**1st Competition Period**
**9th Week**

| TRAINING FEATURE | ORGANISATION/AMOUNT/TIPS |
|---|---|
| **Warm-up:** <br> Jogging | • 20 min – 150 pulse/min <br> • Stretching |
| **Fitness:** <br> Speed <br><br><br><br> Strength endurance | • 30 m sprints <br> • 15 sprints <br> • 30 s break between sprints <br> • 2 x/wk (medium level and above) <br> • "Scuffle ball" (see Program 15) <br> • 20 min |
| **Tactics:** <br> Game critique <br><br><br><br><br> Closing game | • Trainer addresses the tactical mistakes of the last match. <br> Corrections follow during appropriate practice games. <br> • 20-25 min <br><br> • Game 11:11 <br> • Game 8:8 <br> • 30 min |
| **Cool-down:** <br> Slowly walking around | |

# Program 31

**1st Competition Period**
**10th Week**

| TRAINING FEATURE | ORGANISATION/AMOUNT/TIPS |
|---|---|
| **Warm-up:**<br>Game 5:5<br><br>Game 5:2 | • Two ball contacts<br>• 10 min<br>• Direct play<br>• 15 min<br>• Stretching |
| **Technique:**<br>Goal shot<br>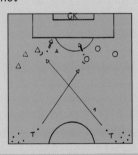 | • After diagonal passes from kick-off circle alternately to two groups, each 25 m in front of the goal. The player who receives the ball stops it and shoots at the goal.<br>• As above – with defenders (medium level and above)<br>• Practice in groups<br>• 20 min |
| **Fitness:**<br>Endurance, leg power, basic speed | • Circuit training<br>Four players always practice together at each station. |

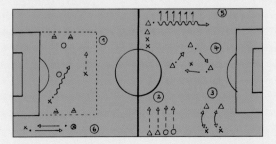

**Station 1**
- Game 2:2 on 40 x 35 m field with small goals

**Station 2**
- 15 m sprints

**Station 3**
- Heading game
- Two partners stand 5 m apart
- One partner throws high balls which the other has to head back while jumping (jumping using both legs)
- After 60 s change roles

**Station 4**
- Game 3:1 on 40 x 35 m field
- The player in the middle can only leave the circle when he has the ball; anyone messing up a pass goes into the circle.

**Station 5**
- Slalom dribbling past 10 poles, 3 m apart

**Station 6**
- Flat passing
- 20 m apart from each other

- Strain:
  120 s max. pace
  60 s break
- 2-3 rounds
- 2 x/wk (top/elite level)
- ca. 30-35 min
- Stretching/loosening exercises
- Slowly running around

**Tactics:**
Teamwork and understanding of the game

- Game 7:5 (midfield and forwards vs. backs)

| | |
|---|---|
| | • The smaller team must try to keep the ball "in its own ranks" as long as possible. |
| | • 25-30 min |
| **Variation:** | • Game 11:11 – free play |
| | • 30-35 min (lower levels) |

**Cool-down:**
Slowly running around

# Program 32

**1st Competition Period**
**10th Week**

| TRAINING FEATURE | ORGANISATION/AMOUNT/TIPS |
|---|---|
| **Warm-up:**<br>Game 3:3 | • Free play<br>• Two ball contacts/player<br>• Direct play<br>• Stretching<br>• 15 min |
| **Fitness:**<br>Speed | • Acceleration with and without ball 15-20 m<br>• 10 x with ball<br>• 10 x without ball<br>• 30 s break after every acceleration<br>• 5-7 min break between series (active ball work)<br>• 2 x/wk (medium level and above) |

**Technique:**
Receiving and taking the ball

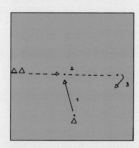

- Group of four
- A player kicks the ball to a sprinting player who must receive it and take it along and in turning kick it back.
- Each player takes turns at kicking the ball to the others.
- 2 x/wk /top lower level and above)
- 20 min

**Tactics:**
Running freely

- Game 4:4 + 1 (neutral player)
- The neutral player always plays with the side that has the ball. The starting team gets away from its covering players immediately after kicking-off, in order to offer itself to the neutral player again (the neutral player may not be covered by the other team).
- Neutral player wears a different colored jersey.

Closing game

- Game 8:8 on half field
- Game 11:11
- 25 min

**Cool-down:**
Slowly running around/stretching

# Program 33

**1st Competition Period**
**11th Week**

| TRAINING FEATURE | ORGANISATION/AMOUNT/TIPS |
|---|---|
| **Warm-up:**<br>Handball/heading with football | • Play according to handball rules; goals can only be scored with headers (playing field 40 x 20 m).<br>• 15 min |
| Game 5:2 | • Direct play<br>• Two ball contacts/player<br>• 15 min |
| **Fitness:**<br>Speed | • 25 m sprints with about turn<br>• 10 x<br>• 30 s break between sprints<br>• 2 x/wk (medium level and above) |
| Endurance specific to soccer | • Game 8:8 on half field<br>• Two ball contacts/player<br>• 2 x/wk (medium level and above)<br>• 20 min |
| **Tactics:**<br>Pressing | • Game 6:6 on half field<br>• Task: On losing the ball in the opponent's half all players move forward and immediately attack the person with the ball while covering the opposing players (see Program 28).<br>• 2 x/wk (medium level and above)<br>• 15-20 min |
| Closing game | • Game 11:11<br>• 20-25 min |
| **Cool-down:**<br>Slowly running around | |

# Program 34

**1st Competition Period
11th Week**

| TRAINING FEATURE | ORGANISATION/AMOUNT/TIPS |
|---|---|
| **Warm-up:** Combining in the penalty area 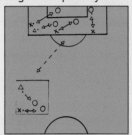 | • Pairs kick the ball back and forth in the penalty area. On the whistle all pairs head for a 15 x 15 square with fast passes and carry on the activity there, etc.<br>• 15 min |
| **Technique:** Flying headers 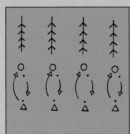 | • Flying headers after ball is thrown, thrower walks backwards and with a short throw requires partner to head the ball back.<br>• 10 x – then role swap<br>• Several series<br>• Only possible on grass field |
| Header in group of four | • Keep the ball in the air with heads only<br>• 10 min |
| Goal shot  | • From the center line<br>• Player stands with back to goal, throws the ball with both hands backwards over his head, sprints after the ball and shoots at the goal. |

- Same set-up as above
- Player juggles the ball, kicks the ball over his head, sprints after it and shoots at the goal.

- Same set-up as above
- Player plays with the trainer until the sudden through pass comes which he must take up and close with a shot at goal.

- Practice in groups
- 25 min

## Tactics:
Moving the game

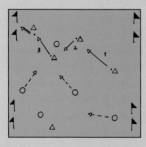

- Game 5:5 on half field with four small goals
- Each team must move the game to the other goal side through skilful team-work and sudden change of direction.
- 2 x/wk (medium level and above)
- Two ball contacts/player (top/elite level)
- 20 min

Closing game

- 11:11 (lower levels)
- 25 min

## Cool-down:
Slowly running/walking around

# Program 35

**1st Competition Period**
**12th Week**

| TRAINING FEATURE | ORGANISATION/AMOUNT/TIPS |
|---|---|
| **Warm-up:**<br>Warm-up running and passing game<br>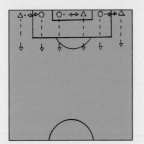 | • In pairs the players begin at the goal out line and pass the ball back and forth.<br>• One field length slow pace<br>• One field length medium pace<br>• Half a field length fast pace<br>• Half a field length slow pace<br><br>• 10 x with short breaks<br>• 15 min<br><br>• Stretching |
| **Technique:**<br>Dribbling | • In pairs the players start from the center line – one partner dribbles forward with the ball, the other gradually moves back and attacks methodically.<br>• Role swap<br>• 10 x/player with short breaks |
| Heading<br>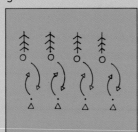 | • Same set-up as above<br>• One partner throws the ball up high, which must be headed back from a jump.<br>• Role swap<br>• 10 x/player<br>• 20 min<br>• 2 x/wk (medium level and above) |

**Fitness:**
Speed endurance

- Fast running – four field lengths
- 5-6 series with complete breaks between

**Variation:**

- Game 4:4
- Two ball contacts/player
- 3 x 5 min max. speed with complete breaks between

**Tactics:**
Closing game

- Game 11:11
- 25 min with the task: The two wingers are only allowed two ball contacts/player (faster goal finish).

**Cool-down:**
Slowly running around

# Program 36

**1st Competition Period**
**12th Week**

| TRAINING FEATURE | ORGANISATION/AMOUNT/TIPS |
| --- | --- |
| **Warm-up:**<br>Jogging | • 10 min |
| Game 5:2 | • 10 min |
| **Fitness:**<br>Speed | • 20 m sprints<br>• 15 x – 30 s break between sprints<br>• 2 x/wk (medium level and above)<br>• Stretching |

**Technique:**

Goal shot

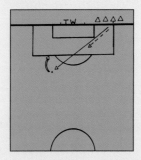

- From a turn
- Two groups stand right and left of the penalty area on the goal out line.
- The ball is played diagonally behind the 16 m line.
- Sprint and shot from the turn.
- Change of position
- 25 min

Playing creativity

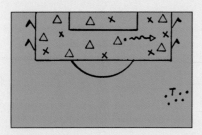

- Game 8:8 in penalty area with small goals
- In a tight space both teams must play technically good football. If the ball rolls over the lines of the penalty area, the trainer immediately throws in another ball.
- 2 x/wk (top lower level and above)
- The number of players can be larger.
- 20 min

**Tactics:**

Closing game

- 11:11
- 7:7 on half field
- 25 min

**Cool-down:**

Slowly running around

# Program 37

**1st Competition Period**
**13th Week**

| TRAINING FEATURE | ORGANISATION/AMOUNT/TIPS |
|---|---|
| **Warm-up:**<br>Rider soccer | • Game 4:4 (with partner piggybacking)<br>• Playing field 20 x 20 m with small goals<br>• Role swap during the game<br>• 15 min |
| Game 5:2 | • Two ball contacts<br>• Direct play<br>• 15 min |
| **Technique:**<br>Individual techniques | • Each player practices his "special tricks"<br>• One ball/player – if not enough balls, group practice possible<br>• Trainer gives tips and ideas<br>• 15 min |
| **Goal shot** | • Free practice<br>• Practice in groups<br>• 20 min |
| Corners | • Specific corner training<br><br>• Ball to first post<br>• Ball to second post<br>• Ball to rear corner of penalty area<br>• Ball to front corner of penalty area<br>• 2 x/wk (medium level and above)<br>• 20 min |

**Fitness:**
Endurance specific to soccer

- Game 7:7 on half field
- Two ball contacts
- Direct play (medium level and above)
- 4 x 5 min with short breaks (Stretching)

**Tactics:**
Closing game

- Game 11:11
- 20 min

Playing for goal opportunities

- Game 5:3 from center line towards goal (two coverers + sweeper vs. five attackers), (medium level and above)
- 25 min

**Cool-down:**
Slowly running around

# Program 38

**1st Competition Period**
**13th Week**

| TRAINING FEATURE | ORGANISATION/AMOUNT/TIPS |
|---|---|
| **Warm-up:** Jogging and stretching | • Run around a marked rectangle 70 x 40 m <br> • 10 min with short breaks and stretching |
| Game 5:2 | • Two ball contacts <br> • Direct play <br> • 10 min |
| **Fitness:** Endurance | • Endurance run – 160 pulse/min <br> • 25-30 min ("strain reminder," see Chapter 6 – Training Periodization) |

Speed
Acceleration with and without ball

- The players form up at the center line without a ball.
- At the whistle they accelerate briefly and about turn.
- 3-5 x

- As above – with ball
- 3-5 x
- Stretching

**Tactics:**
Covering the field

- Game 5:3
- On the center line four mini-goals are set up, which the group of three plays to. The group of five plays to the large goal and two small goals beside it on the goal out line.
- Task: The group of five should narrow down the available space by "pushing" to the side close to the ball.

- The person in the group of three who has the ball should always be attacked by two opponents at once.
- 2 x/wk (medium level and above)
- 25 min

Game critique

- Correction of mistakes from the last championship game

Closing game

- Game 11:11
- Game 7:7 on half field with small goals
- 25 min

**Cool-down:**
Slowly running around

# Program 39

**1st Competition Period**
**14th Week**

| TRAINING FEATURE | ORGANISATION/AMOUNT/TIPS |
|---|---|
| **Warm-up:**<br>Game 5:2 | • Two ball contacts<br>• Direct play<br>• 15 min |
| Game with small goals | • Game 4:4 with small goals<br>• Free play<br>• Stretching<br>• 15 min |
| **Technique:**<br>Dribbling and feinting | • Game 1:1 with small goals<br>• Role swap after successful goal shot |
| | |
| | • Game 6:6 outside the penalty area<br>• Task: The attackers must penetrate the penalty area and shoot at the goal (the defenders may only defend outside the penalty area).<br>• Role swap<br>• 2 x/wk (medium level and above)<br>• 25 min |

**Fitness:**
Speed

- 20 m sprints
- 15 x - 30 s break between sprints
- 2 x/wk (medium level and above)

**Variation:**

- With ball and about turn

**Tactics:**
Securing the ball

- Game 6:6 on half field
- Each team places a man on the sideline who moves up and down and should be played to by his own team as often as possible.
- Each time he is played to a point is earned.

**Variation:**

- Person playing to him must do so directly.
- Role swap
- 20 min

**Cool-down:**
Slowly running around

# Program 40

**1st Competition Period**
**14th Week**

| TRAINING FEATURE | ORGANISATION/AMOUNT/TIPS |
|---|---|
| **Warm-up:**<br>Medicine ball game in penalty area | • Two players carrying medicine balls chase their team-mates and try to tag these with the ball; whoever is tagged takes over the ball and becomes a chaser.<br>• 10-15 min |
| **Tactics:**<br>Pressing<br><br><br><br>Game critique | • Game 5+1 (GK) vs. four (attackers) + one neutral player<br>• Task: The larger team must constantly attack whoever has the ball with two players.<br>• Deliberate back passes to player placed further back force the defense to run more (move play).<br>• 2 x/wk (medium level and above)<br>• 25 min<br>• Loosening exercises<br>• Correction of mistakes made in last game |
| **Fitness:**<br>Endurance specific to soccer | • Game 6:6 on half field<br>• Two ball contacts/player<br>• Direct play (top/elite level)<br>• 3 x 7 min mit short breaks |
| **Variation:**<br>Goal shooting as fitness exercise | • Free practice<br>• 20 min |
| **Cool-down:**<br>Slowly running around and stretching | |

# Program 41

**1st Competition Period**
**15th Week**

| TRAINING FEATURE | ORGANISATION/AMOUNT/TIPS |
|---|---|
| **Warm-up:**<br>Game 4:2 | In marked rectangle<br>• Two ball contacts for the group of four, free play for the group of two<br>• 15 min<br>• Stretching |
| **Technique:**<br>Goal shot | • After double pass play<br>• With opponent |
| | • After center pass from right and left<br>• With opponent<br>• Practice in groups<br>• 2 x/wk (top/elite level)<br>• 25 min<br>• Slowly running around |
| **Fitness:**<br>Speed | • 20 m sprints<br>• 15 x – 30 s break between sprints<br>• 2 x/wk (medium level and above) |

**Tactics:**
Shifting play

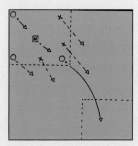

- Game 3:3 + "Neutral player" in a 20 x 25 m rectangle with the task: Play to the neutral player as often as possible. After five ball contacts with the neutral player play can be shifted to the other free rectangle with a diagonal pass. All players immediately move there.
- The neutral player may not be attacked.

- 20 min

**Variation:**

- Trainer gives the signal to change fields.
- Two ball contacts/player
- 2 x/wk (medium level and above)

Closing game

- Game 11:11
- 25 min

**Cool-down:**
Slowly running around

# Program 42

**1st Competition Period**
**15th Week**

| TRAINING FEATURE | ORGANISATION/AMOUNT/TIPS |
|---|---|
| **Warm-up:**<br>Running with changes of pace | • Warm-up running around the field<br>• Hopping gait<br>• Side gallop<br>• On the heels<br>• Skipping<br>• Jumps with half turn<br>• Jumps with header<br>• Running backwards<br>• Trainer announces change<br>• 15 min<br>• Stretching and loosening |
| **Fitness:**<br>Speed with the ball | • 20 m sprints with the ball<br>• 15 x – 30 s break between sprints<br>• 2 x/wk (medium level and higher) |
| Endurance specific to soccer | • Game 5:5<br>• Two ball contacts/player<br>• 4 x 5 min with complete breaks (active ball work)<br>• 2 x/wk (top/elite level) |
| **Tactics:**<br>Game without ball  | • Game 4:4 + four "neutrals"<br>• On a 35 x 40 m field four "neutrals" stand in a corner and should be played to as often as possible by the team in possession of the ball.<br>• Role swap after 5 min. |

| | |
|---|---|
| | • The "neutrals" become a new team while the other team members become "neutrals." |
| | • 20 min |
| **Variation:** | • With limited contacts for the playing teams |
| | • Back passes to the "neutrals" are not allowed. |
| Closing game | • Game 11:11 |
| | • 25 min (lower levels) |
| **Cool-down:** Slowly walking around/stretching | |

# Program 43

**1st Competition Period**
**16th Week**

| TRAINING FEATURE | ORGANISATION/AMOUNT/TIPS |
|---|---|
| **Warm-up:** Game 5:2 | • Two ball contacts/player |
| | • Direct play |
| | • 10 min |
| Ball control in penalty area | • Each player moves the ball at his feet. |
| | • Trainer announces change of pace: turns; stops; change of foot etc. |
| | • 10 min |
| | • Stretching |
| **Technique:** Individual techniques | • Free, creative practice |
| | • One ball/player |

| Heading | • In pairs |
| | • 10 min |

**Goal shot**

• After center pass against one defender and goal keeper.
• Three attackers stand outside the penalty area and await the center pass for a shot at goal.
• Keep playing until a goal can be shot.
• 20-25 min
• 2 x/wk (medium level and above)

**Variation:**

• As above
• With two defenders

**Tactics:**

Game critique

• Correction of mistakes from last championship match

Closing game

• Game 11:11
• Game 7:7 on half field
• 20 min

**Cool-down:**

Slowly running around

# Program 44

**1st Competition Period**
**16th Week**

| TRAINING FEATURE | ORGANISATION/AMOUNT/TIPS |
|---|---|
| **Warm-up:** Playing the ball while running | • Three players line up 10 m apart on the goal out line and play and keep playing the ball to each other as far as the other side.<br>• 10-15 x/group of three |
| Game 5:2 | • Group of five may only play with the "weak" foot<br>• 15 min<br><br>• Stretching |
| **Fitness:** Endurance specific to soccer | • Game 2:2:2 with small goals<br>• One team always takes a break and jogs.<br>• 5-7 x 2 min max. playing speed |
| **Tactics:** Playing for goal opportunities | • Game 6:6 + three "neutrals":<br>• The neutral players may only play directly and may not score goals. |

| | |
|---|---|
| | • After each round the "neutrals" change. |
| | • 4 x 5 min with short breaks |
| | • 2 x/wk (medium level and above) |
| Closing game | • Game 11:11 |
| | • 25 min |

**Cool-down:**
Slowly running around

# Program 45

**2nd Preparational Period (if a winterbreak is taken)**
**1st Week**

| TRAINING FEATURE | ORGANISATION/AMOUNT/TIPS |
|---|---|
| **Warm-up:**<br>Jogging and stretching | • On the field<br>• 15 min |
| **Fitness:**<br>Basic endurance | • Cross-country run<br>• 5-7 km – 160 pulse/minute<br>• At the beginning of the preparation for the replay round endurance is trained so that the players can compensate the loss of fitness during the winter break as quickly as possible.<br>• 2 x/wk (medium level and higher)<br>• C 25-30 min |

**Technique:**

Individual techniques

- Each player practices with a ball and practices his personal ball skills.
- 2 x/wk (top lower level and above)
- 15-20 min

Goal shot

- Free practice
- In groups
- 20 min

**Tactics:**

Majority vs. minority

- Game 5:3 on half field from the center line. If the group of three gets possession, the ball must be played back to the center line.

- Two ball contacts
- Free play
- 2 x/wk (medium level and above)
- 25 min

**Cool-down:**

Slowly running around

# Program 46

**2nd Preparational Period**
**1st Week**

| TRAINING FEATURE | ORGANISATION/AMOUNT/TIPS |
|---|---|
| **Warm-up:**<br>Handball/soccer alternating | • Game 6:6 on half field<br>• The game starts with soccer, but during the game it can be continued as handball. Goals can be scored with hands, feet and head.<br>• 15 min<br>• Stretching |
| **Fitness:**<br>Basic endurance | • Cross-country running<br>• 5-7 km – 160 pulse/min<br>• On the 400 m track or around the field<br>• 2 x/wk (medium level and above)<br>• c. 25-30 min |
| **Technique:**<br>Goal shot | • Game 3:2 on a limited field<br>• Only goals shot from within the penalty area count. After a successfully completed attack the attackers return to the center circle.<br>• 2 x/wk (medium level and above)<br>• Practice in groups<br>• 25 min |

**Tactics:**
Shifting the play

- Game 7:7 + two "neutrals" on playing field between the two penalty areas
  The neutrals act as wall players who are only allowed to play through passes. Skilfull free movement and occupying the areas in time are required.
- 2 x/wk (medium level and above)

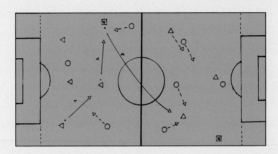

**Variation:**

- Complete field and goal shooting
- 25 min

**Cool-down:**
Slowly running around/stretching

# Program 47

**2nd Preparational Period**
**2nd Week**

| TRAINING FEATURE | ORGANISATION/AMOUNT/TIPS |
|---|---|
| **Warm-up:**<br>Jogging | • 5 min |
| **Fitness:**<br>Basic endurance<br><br><br><br>Speed | • Cross-country running<br>• 5-7 km – 160 pulse/min<br>• c. 25-30 min<br>• Stretching<br>• 15 m sprints<br>• 15 x – 30 s break between sprints<br>• 2 x/wk (top lower level and above) |
| **Technique:**<br>Corners<br><br>Penalty<br><br>Free kick | • Free practice<br>• Practice in groups<br>• Free practice<br>• Practice in groups<br>• Free practice<br>• Practice in groups<br>• 2 x/wk (medium level and above)<br>• 25 min |
| **Tactics:**<br>Game without ball<br> | • Game 4:4 with small goals<br>• Playing field 20 x 40 m (penalty area)<br>• Two ball contacts<br>• Direct play<br>• 5 x 3 min with short breaks |
| **Cool-down:**<br>Slowly running around | |

# Program 48

**2nd Preparational Period**
**2nd Week**

| TRAINING FEATURE | ORGANISATION/AMOUNT/TIPS |
| --- | --- |
| **Warm-up:**<br>Game 5:2 | • Two ball contacts<br>• Direct play<br>• 10 min |
| **Fitness:**<br>Speed | • 3 x 10 accelerations<br>• After each series complete recovery (active ball work) |
| **Variation:** | • With ball |
| **Technique:**<br>Individual techniques | • Juggling the ball with foot, thigh, head<br>• On the spot<br>• While moving<br>• With partner |

- Ball control with feints, stops, turns, changes of pace, etc.
- Play the ball high
- Stop with foot, thigh, chest

- 2 x/wk (lower levels)
- 15-20 min

**Goal shot**

- Free practice
- 2 x/wk (top lower level and above)
- 20 min

**Tactics:**
Change of playing ryhthm

- Game 6:6 on half field
- Trainer determines which player/s play/s directly or must keep the ball. All other players are only allowed two ball contacts.

- 2 x/wk (medium level and above)
- 20 min

Closing game

- Game 11:11
- 20 min (lower levels)

**Cool-down:**
Slowly running around

# Program 49

**2nd Preparational Period**
**3rd Week**

| TRAINING FEATURE | ORGANISATION/AMOUNT/TIPS |
| --- | --- |

**Warm-up:**
Scuffle ball

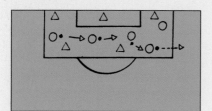

- Two teams with 5-8 players try to carry a medicine ball across the "goal line" of the penalty area through fast direct passing to each other. Physical activity may only be directed at the ball, not other players.
- 15 min

**Technique:**
Dribbling and feinting

- Two partners practise together
- "Sole trick" – Dribbling parallel to the sideline, pretend to offer the ball to the opponent; with the sole quickly pull it back and take it round 90° to the direction run in with the instep.

- Ditto, but only begin the deception and using the inside of the foot take the ball in the same direction.

- "Stan Mathews Trick"
- Ball is taken to the left with the instep (body weight on the back leg) and suddenly dribbled away to the right.

- 10 x/player – then role swap
- 2-3 series
- 2 x/wk (top lower level and above)
- c. 20 min

**Fitness:**

Endurance specific to soccer

- Game 6:6 on half field
- Two ball contacts
- 5-7 x 3 min with short breaks
- Stretching

**Tactics:**

Covering the field

- Game 5:3 (see Program 38)
- 2 x/wk (medium level and above)
- 25 min

Closing game

- Game 11:11
- 20 min

**Cool-down:**

Slowly running around/loosening exercises

# Program 50

**2nd Preparational Period**
**3rd Week**

| TRAINING FEATURE | ORGANISATION/AMOUNT/TIPS |
|---|---|
| **Warm-up:**<br>Skipping and stretching | • One skipping rope/player<br>• Skipping with both feet and jump in between<br>• Ditto without jump in between<br>• On one leg with jump in between<br>• Ditto without jump in between<br><br>• Alternating jump right/left with jump in between<br>• Ditto without jump in between<br>• Stretching<br>• 15 min |
| **Fitness:**<br>Speed with the ball<br><br>**Variation:**<br><br><br>Ability to jump and strength endurance<br><br> | • 25 m sprints with ball<br>• 15 x – 30 s break between sprints<br>• As a chase with partner (line up 1 m apart from man in front)<br><br>• Jump with header<br>• Partner throws a high ball which the other heads back from a jump.<br><br>• 10 x<br>• 3-5 series – with role swap<br><br>• Ditto with weight jacket (10-15% of body weight)<br>• c. 25 min<br>• Afterwards, loosening exercises |

**Tactics:**
Forechecking

- Game 11:11 with the task:
  Play "forechecking" – the opposing team is attacked 20 m behind the center line. Several players attack the player with the ball, the midfield players follow in order to prevent countering efforts of the opponents. The defenders cover the forwards closely. The sweeper secures.

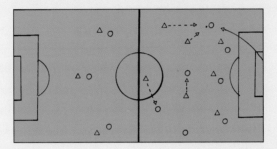

- 2 x/wk (medium level and above)
- Trainer gives commands for "fore-checking" at the beginning.

- 25-30 min

**Cool-down:**
Slowly running around/stretching

# Program 51

**2nd Preparational Period**
**4th Week**

| TRAINING FEATURE | ORGANISATION/AMOUNT/TIPS |
|---|---|
| **Warm-up:**<br>Controlling the ball | • Controlling the ball with direction changes, stops, about turns, pace changes, juggling the ball etc.<br>• 15 min<br>• Stretching |
| **Technique:**<br>Passing with side on the ball<br> | • Two partners stand 20 m apart and kick the ball back and forth with side on it.<br>• Flat pass<br>• Half high balls<br>• High balls |
| Free kick with side | • Ditto |
| Corner with side | • Ditto<br>• 25 min |
| **Fitness:**<br>Speed endurance | • Intensified running across whole field<br>• 6 x 3 runs<br>• 3 min break after each series<br>• 2 x/wk (top/elite level)<br>• c. 25 min<br>• 5 min slowly running around |

**Tactics:**
Majority vs. minority

- Game 3:3 + two "neutrals:" The two "neutrals" always play with the team in possession in order to create an outnumbering team in each case.

- 2x/wk (medium level and above)

- 15 min − with short breaks

**Variations:**

- Ditto with small goals

Closing game

- Game 11:11 (lower levels)
- 25 min

**Cool-down:**
Slowly running around

# Program 52

**2nd Preparational Period
4th Week**

| TRAINING FEATURE | ORGANISATION/AMOUNT/TIPS |
|---|---|
| **Warm-up:**<br>Chain tag | <ul><li>A hunter begins the hunt in the penalty area, where all players are located. He tries to tag a player, who then works with him (hands linked) to tag the next one. Once four players are together, the "chain" is divided into two pairs. etc.</li><li>The other players may not leave the penalty area.</li></ul> |

- 10-15 min
- Stretching

## Fitness:
Acceleration speed

- The players pass to a goal keeper 15 m away and run as fast as they can towards the ball after he has thrown it and bring it under control.
- 15 x/player

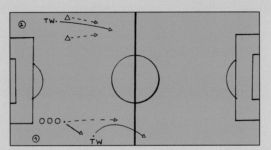

- Line up in pairs at the center line
- Trainer throws a ball in the direction of the penalty area, towards which both run.
- Ditto as flat pass
- Ditto as high ball
- 10 x/player pair
- Slowly running around

## Tactics:
Crossing over before the opposing defense

- Game 5:5 on half field from the center line to the big goal
- The two wings of the attacking party try to cross over before the penalty area. If the defense gets possession, a new attack begins from the center line.

- Wings detach themselves very quickly and run diagonally
- Role swap – defense attacks and vice versa
- 2 x/wk (medium level and above)
- 25 min

Closing game
- Game 11:11
- 25 min

**Cool-down:**
Slowly running around/loosening exerxcises

# Program 53

**2nd Competition Period**
**1st Week**

| TRAINING FEATURE | ORGANISATION/AMOUNT/TIPS |
| --- | --- |
| **Warm-up:**<br>Game 3:1 | • Two ball contacts<br>• The player who passes incorrectly must go in the middle.<br>• 15 min<br>• Stretching |
| **Fitness:**<br>Endurance specific to soccer | • All players dribble, under instruction from the trainer, on a 20 x 30 m field.<br>• Relaxed dribbling (3-4 min)<br>• Dribbling at increased pace and with many direction changes (2-3 min)<br><br>• Feinting with short accelerations (10 m)<br>• Slow dribbling onto other field<br>• In doing so, keeping ball high, stopping etc. |

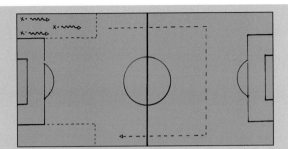

- 5-7 series with short breaks
- 25-30 min
- Stretching

**Tactics:**
Counter play

- Through passing as a means of fast countering
- Game 5:5 on half field with small goals. At the trainer's whistle the team in possession tries to score with a through pass to the large goal. After that the game carries on across the broad side.

- 2 x/wk (medium level and above)
- 20 min

**Cool-down:**
Slowly running around/stretching

# Program 54

**2nd Competition Period**
**1st Week**

| TRAINING FEATURE | ORGANISATION/AMOUNT/TIPS |
|---|---|
| **Warm-up:**<br>Jogging/Stretching | • 10 min |
| **Fitness:**<br>Speed | • 20 m sprints<br>• 15 x – 30 s break between sprints |
| Endurance specific to soccer | • Game 5:5 on half field<br>• Two ball contacts/player<br>• 4 x 5 min with short breaks |
| **Technique:**<br>Goal shot  | • After bouncing off the trainer. The players stand with the ball in the center circle and after brief dribbling play to the trainer, who lets the ball bounce off sideways, to be kicked at goal by the player.<br>• Let players practice from right and left |
| Goal shot | • After bouncing off the trainer. The players stand on the sideline on the level of the penalty area, play to the trainer, who lets the ball bounce back, and shoot at goal.<br>• Let players practice from right and left<br><br>• 20 min |

**Tactics:**

Game overview and understanding of game

- Game 4:4 with an open goal on a marked field between the two penalty areas with a side corridor each. One team begins and tries to score a goal through skilful passing. If the ball goes past the goal, the other team gets possession. The team in possession must try to keep the ball long enough for a player to get in position to shoot for goal.
- Further teams of four run up and down in the corridor until it is their turn.
- Change every 5 min

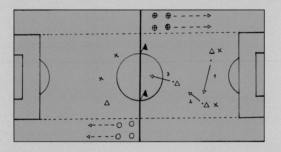

- c. 25 min

- 2 x/wk (medium level and above)

Closing game

- Game 11:11 (only lower levels)
- 25 min

**Cool-down:**

Slowly running around

# Program 55

**2nd Competition Period**
**2nd Week**

| TRAINING FEATURE | ORGANISATION/AMOUNT/TIPS |
|---|---|
| **Warm-up:**<br>Running and ball control | • The players warm-up by running with a ball at their feet.<br>• 15 min<br>• Stretching |
| **Fitness:**<br>Speed | • Line sprints with about turn<br>• All players line up on the goal out line.<br>1. Sprint to 5 m line and back<br>2. Sprint to 11 m line and back<br>3. Sprint to 16 m line and back<br>• 5 series<br>• Complete breaks between series<br><br>• 2 x/wk (medium level and above) |
| **Technique:**<br>Individual techniques | • Each player practices with a ball, trains his feeling for the ball and improves his ball handling.<br>• 15 min |
| **Tactics:**<br>Covering | • Game 4:4 – each player is assigned a man to cover by the trainer.<br>• Free play<br>• Two ball contacts/player<br>• Direct play /top/elite level)<br>• 2 x/wk (medium level and above)<br>• 15 min with short breaks |

| Closing game | • Game 11:11 |
| | • 25 min |

**Cool-down:**
Slowly running around/loosening exercises

# Program 56

**2nd Competition Period**
**2nd Week**

| TRAINING FEATURE | ORGANISATION/AMOUNT/TIPS |
| --- | --- |
| **Warm-up:**<br>Game 4:2 | • Group of four has two ball contacts/ player<br>• Group of two can dribble<br>• 15 min<br>• Stretching |
| **Technique:**<br>Feeling for the ball<br><br> | • Practice in groups of four<br>• Quick flat passes with change of position<br>• Passing and accepting half high balls<br>• Heading to others and changing position<br>• 2 x/wk (lower levels)<br>• 15 min |
| **Fitness:**<br>General strengthening | • Playful practicing with partner<br>• Juggling the ball while sitting<br>• Two partners sit opposite each other and pass the ball back and forth |

- Sprints against an elastic band
- One partner sprints against an elastic band attached to the railing

- Throwing the ball while doing press-ups
- Two partners throw the ball back and forth while doing one-arm push-ups.

- One legged knee bends
- Two partners hold each other's right foot and left hand
- Sink to a 90° position and stand up again.

- Arm wrestling standing on one leg
- Two partners clasp hands and try to put the other off balance so he has to lower his "free" foot.
- Repeat each exercise several times.

- c. 20 min

**Tactics:**
Understanding the game and game overview

- Game 7:7:7 on 3/4 field (penalty area to penalty area)
- One team always has a break and jogs
- 25 min

**Variation:**

- Game 8:8:8 with two ball contacts/player (medium level and above)
- 25 min

**Cool-down:**
Slowly running around

# Program 57

**2nd Competition Period**
**3rd Week**

| TRAINING FEATURE | ORGANISATION/AMOUNT/TIPS |
| --- | --- |
| **Warm-up:**<br>Game 5:2 | • Two ball contacts<br>• Direct play<br>• 15 min |
| **Technique:**<br>Goal shot | • After a pass against a defender<br>• Three players stand at the center line and play to their team partners, who are covered. By dribbling the recipient gets past the coverer and shoots at the goal.<br><br>• Role swap<br>• 2 x/wk (medium level and above)<br>• 25 min |
| **Fitness:**<br>Strength endurance | • "Rider soccer" with small goals (one partner carries the other piggyback)<br>• Game 5:5 on a 40 x 20 m field (penalty area)<br>• Role swap as often as desired<br>• 20 min |
| **Tactics:**<br>Forechecking | • Game 11:11 (see Program 50)<br>• 2 x/wk (medium level and above)<br>• 25 min |
| **Cool-down:**<br>Slowly running around/loosening exercises | |

# Program 58

**2nd Competition Period**
**3rd Week**

| TRAINING FEATURE | ORGANISATION/AMOUNT/TIPS |
|---|---|
| **Warm-up:**<br>Jogging and stretching | • 15 min |
| **Technique:**<br>Individual techniques | • "Soccer tennis" on a 15 x 15 m field<br>• Four players play together<br>• As many contacts as desired in one's own half<br>• Net height 1.5 m |
| **Variation:** | • Three ball contacts in one's own half<br>• 15 min |
| **Tactics:**<br>Covering a man in difficult situations | • Game 4:4 + 1 with close covering<br>• One player additionally covers the opponent with the ball who must thus get past two covering opponents.<br>• 2 x/wk (medium level and above)<br>• Two ball contacts/player<br>• 20 min with short breaks |
| **Fitness:**<br>Endurance specific to soccer | • Game 7:7 on half field<br>• 2 x/wk (top lower level and above)<br>• Two ball contacts/player<br>• 4 x 5 min with short breaks<br>• Stretching/loosening exercises |
| **Cool-down:**<br>Slowly running around | |

# Program 59

**2nd Competition Period**
**4th Week**

| TRAINING FEATURE | ORGANISATION/AMOUNT/TIPS |
|---|---|
| **Warm-up:**<br>Running and controlling the ball | • Trainer determines pace, change of direction, stops etc.<br>• 15 min<br>• Stretching |
| **Technique:**<br>Indirect free kick | • After playing away with the heel<br>• Three players stand ready. Player 1 pretends to play to 2, but plays it to 3 with his heel, who shoots at goal. |
| Direct free kick | • Free kick with side around the wall<br>• The players chosen for free kicks practice<br>• 2 x/wk (medium level and above)<br>• 25 min |
| **Fitness:**<br>Speed endurance | • Interval running in a marked rectangle (50 x 30 m)<br><br>• One round at medium pace<br>• One round at fast pace<br>• One round at slow pace<br>• One round at top speed<br>• One round at slow pace |

| | |
|---|---|
| | • 3-5 series |
| | • 3 min break between series |
| | • c. 20-25 min |
| **Tactics:** | |
| Shifting the game | • Game 7:7 + two "neutrals" (see Program 46) |
| | • 2 x/wk (medium level and above) |
| | • 25 min |
| Closing game | • Game 11:11 |
| | • 25 min |
| **Cool-down:** | |
| Slowly running around | |

# Program 60

**2nd Competition Period**
**4th Week**

| TRAINING FEATURE | ORGANISATION/AMOUNT/TIPS |
|---|---|
| **Warm-up:** | |
| Game 5:2 | • Two ball contacts |
| | • Direct play |
| | • 15 min |
| | • Stretching |
| **Fitness:** | |
| Speed | • 20 m sprints |
| | • 15 x 30 s break between sprints |
| | • 2 x/wk (medium level and above) |
| **Technique:** | |
| Heading | • As goal shot after center pass from right and left |

- Practicing as above
- Trainer throws the ball to player sprinting towards him so he can head it back.
- 2 x/wk (top lower level and higher)
- 20 min

## Tactics:

Indirect free kick

- Lobbed free kick in front of penalty area
- Five players form a wall
- Player 1 pretends to play to player 2 and lifts the ball over the wall. Player 3 dashes past the wall and shoots at goal.

- 2 x/wk (medium level and above)
- 15 min

Closing game

- 11:11
- 6:6 on half field
- 25 min

## Cool-down:

Slowly running around

# Program 61

**2nd Competition Period**
**5th Week**

| TRAINING FEATURE | ORGANISATION/AMOUNT/TIPS |
|---|---|
| **Warm-up:**<br>Game 4:2 | • Team of four two ball contacts/player<br>• Team of two free play<br>• 15 min |
| **Technique:**<br>Dribbling<br><br> | • Dribbling 1 +1:1 on the wing<br>• On each side of the field are a starter player, a forward and a defender. In the penalty area two attackers work against a covering man. The two forwards, alternating right and left and working with the appropriate starter player must penetrate past the defender and center pass towards the two players in the penalty area.<br>• 2 x/wk (medium level and above)<br>• Role swap after several dribblings<br>• 25 min |
| **Tactics/Fitness:**<br>Game without a ball | • Game 5:5 on half field with small goals<br>• Two ball contacts/player<br>• Direct play (medium level and above)<br>• 2 x/wk (medium level and above)<br>• 20 min |
| **Cool-down:**<br>Slowly running around | |

# Program 62

**2nd Competition Period
5th Week**

| TRAINING FEATURE | ORGANISATION/AMOUNT/TIPS |
|---|---|
| **Warm-up:**<br>Jogging and stretching | • 15 min |
| **Technique:**<br>Individual techniques | • Game 3:3 with small goals<br>• Players may only play with the "weak" foot<br>• On breaking this rule – change of ball possession<br>• 2 x/wk (top lower level and above)<br>• 15 min |
| Goal shot | • Free practicing as players choose<br>• Practicing in groups<br>• 20 min |
| **Fitness:**<br>Speed | • 25 m sprints<br>• 10 x – 30 s break between sprints<br>• 2 x/wk (medium level and above) |
| **Tactics:**<br>Majority vs. minority<br> | • Game 5:5 + two "neutrals" who always play with the team in possession.<br>• Every player is a "neutral" once.<br>• 20 min |
| **Cool-down:**<br>Slowly running around/stretching | |

# Program 63

**2nd Competition Period**
**6th Week**

| TRAINING FEATURE | ORGANISATION/AMOUNT/TIPS |
|---|---|
| **Warm-up:**<br>Warm-up running with the ball | • One ball/player<br>• Trainer gives instructions about how to handle the ball, e.g. slowly, quickly, with stops and about turns, slalom dribbling, keeping the ball high, playing ahead and pulling back with the sole, 1/2 and complete turns, etc.<br>• 15 min without major breaks |
| **Technique:**<br>Center passing | • Center passing from right and left<br><br>• Center passing after dribbling 1:1 along the sideline |

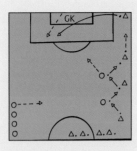

- Center passing after double pass
- Practice in groups
- 2 x/wk (medium level and above)
- 20 min

**Fitness/Tactics:**
Endurance specific to soccer

- Game 6:6 on half field with the task After losing the ball in the opponent's half immediately run back into own half and occupy the areas designated beforehand (division of space)
- 2 x/wk (medium level and above)
- 25 min

**Cool-down:**
Slowly running around

# Program 64

**2nd Competition Period
6th Week**

| TRAINING FEATURE | ORGANISATION/AMOUNT/TIPS |
| --- | --- |
| **Warm-up:**<br>Game 5:2 | - Two ball contacts/player<br>- Direct play<br>- 15 min<br>- Stretching |

**Technique:**
Goal shot

- Outplay goalkeeper
- Start from center line

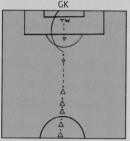

- Lobbed free kick
- Goalkeeper stands 5-7 m in front of his goal. Players begin c. 30 m in front of goal, feint a shot and complete with a high ball.

Penalty

- Each player shoots a penalty
- 25 min

**Fitness:**
Endurance

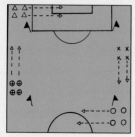

- Speed running around the marked rectangle 35 x 70 m

- Long side medium pace, short side slowly

- Long side fast, short side slowly

- Short side fast, long side medium
- 5-7 series
- 3-5 min break between series

**Tactics:**

Setting-up

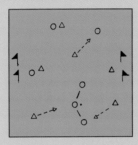

- Game 6:6 on half field with the task: The player with the ball should have at least two more players directly near him (majority with the ball)
- 2 x/wk (top lower level and above)
- 25 min

Closing game

- 11:11 (lower levels)
- 25 min

**Cool-down:**

Slowly running around/loosening exercises

# Program 65

**2nd Competition Period**
**7th Week**

| TRAINING FEATURE | ORGANISATION/AMOUNT/TIPS |
|---|---|
| **Warm-up:**<br>Jogging and stretching | • 15 min |
| **Fitness:**<br>Acceleration speed | • Acceleration with a number of variations<br><br>• From lying on one's back<br>• After skipping on the spot<br>• After a jump with a complete turn<br>• From lying on one's stomach<br>• From a crouch<br>• From a press-up<br>• After jumping and clapping one's hands over one's head (jumping jack)<br>• From a straddle jump<br>• From crossover – ahead/behind<br>• After hopping on one leg<br>• 2-3 series<br>• 3-5 min break between series |
| **Technique:**<br>Dribbling | • Game 1 + 2 vs. 2 + 1:<br>• One neutral player on each side of a limited playing field plays with the group in ball possession. Through dribbling and teamwork the attackers must get past the defenders.<br>• 2 x/wk (top lower level and above)<br>• Independently decide role swap<br>• 20 min |

**Goal shot**

- Free practicing
- Practice in groups
- 15 min

**Tactics:**

Attack against a strengthened defense

- Game 3:5 (three forwards vs. five defenders) with large goal
- After successful defense or goal a new attack begins at the center line.
- 20 min

Closing game

- Game 11:11 (lower levels only)
- 20 min

**Cool-down:**

Slowly running around

# Program 66

**2nd Competition Period**
**7th Week**

| TRAINING FEATURE | ORGANISATION/AMOUNT/TIPS |
|---|---|
| **Warm-up:**<br>Game 5:2 | • Two ball contacts/player<br>• Direct play<br>• 15 min |
| **Technique:**<br>Individual techniques | • Each player practices his own special tricks<br>• Practice feints<br>• Keeping the ball high on the spot and moving<br>• Control ball in penalty area<br>• 15 min |
| Goal shot<br> | • After dribbling and center pass: Two groups line up near the center line. A player from Group A dribbles towards a defender; just before reaching him he passes to a player from Group B who has crossed behind his back towards the outside and who then center passes to the player from A.<br><br>• 2 x/wk (medium level and above)<br>• 25 min |
| **Fitness:**<br>Endurance specific to soccer | • Game 6:6 + one "neutral" on half field<br>• The "neutral" plays with the team in possession. |

Two ball contacts/player
- Direct play (medium level and above)
- 20 min

---

**Tactics:**

Correction of mistakes from last match
- Game forms designed to eradicate tactical shortcomings
- Medium level and above only

Closing game
- Game 11:11 (lower levels only)
- 20 min

---

**Cool-down:**

Loosening exercises

---

# Program 67

**2nd Competition Period**
**8th Week**

| TRAINING FEATURE | ORGANISATION/AMOUNT/TIPS |
| --- | --- |
| **Warm-up:**<br>Partner exercises with the ball | • Flat passing<br>• One throws the ball, partner heads it back.<br>• One throws the ball ahead with a high throw, the other runs to stop it.<br>• One runs backwards and must return passes. |

- One runs backwards and must head back the ball when thrown to him.
- Three series, partners exchange roles.

**Fitness:**

Speed

- 25 m sprints
- 10 x – 30 s break between sprints
- Two series
- Complete break between series with stretching
- 2 x/wk (medium level and above)

**Tactics:**

Playing on the wing

- Game 8:8 on whole field:
- Between penalty area and center line, on each side of the center line, mini-goals are set-up with markers. The team in possession has to play through them in order to reach the main goal and score.

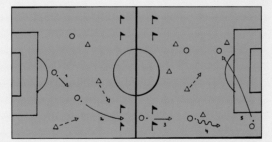

- If the attack does not go through one of the two mini-goals, the other team gets the ball.

- 2 x/wk (medium level and above)
- 25-30 min

Closing game

- game 11:11 (lower levels only)
- 30 min

**Cool-down:**

Slowly running around

# Program 68

**2nd Competition Period**
**8th Week**

| TRAINING FEATURE | ORGANISATION/AMOUNT/TIPS |
|---|---|
| **Warm-up:**<br>Game 4:2 | • Group of four has two ball contacts/player<br>• Group of two can dribble<br>• 15 min<br>• Stretching |
| **Fitness:**<br>Endurance specific to soccer | • Game 6:6 on half field<br>• Two ball contacts/player<br>• Direct play /top/elite level)<br>• 3 x 10 min with short breaks<br>• 2 x/wk (top/elite level) |
| **Tactics:**<br>Securing the ball | • Game 6:6 on half field with small goals:<br>• Through confident short passes and fast running around the field, each team tries to keep the ball in its "own ranks" for as long as possible.<br>• 2 x/wk (medium level and above)<br>• 25 min |
| Closing game | • 11:11<br>• In own half as many ball contacts/player as desired<br>• In opponent's half two ball contacts/player<br>• 20 min (lower levels only) |
| **Cool-down:**<br>Slowly running around | |

# Program 69

**2nd Competition Period**
**9th Week**

| TRAINING FEATURE | ORGANISATION/AMOUNT/TIPS |
|---|---|
| **Warm-up:**<br>Jogging and stretching | • 15 min |
| **Technique:**<br>Accepting and moving the ball<br>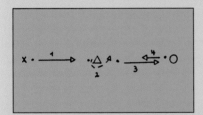<br>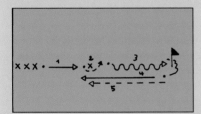 | • Two partners play the ball to each other; the accepting player does a half turn and plays the ball to a third player who plays it back, half turn, pass, etc.<br><br>• Group of four – three players line up. The fourth player stands about 15 m away, accepts the ball played to him, dribbles around a marker and passes it back to the group then goes to the back of the line. The second player from the group runs to replace him.<br><br>• 3-5 series/practice<br>• 25 min |
| **Goal shot**<br>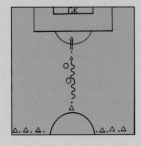 | • After successfully dribbling past two defenders<br>• As above with double pass<br><br>• 2 x/wk (top lower level and above)<br>• 20 min |

**Fitness:**

Endurance

- 5,000 m run as "strain reminder"
- c. 25 min

**Tactics:**

Majority vs. minority

- Game 5:5 + one "neutral" who always plays with the team in possession.

- 2 x/wk (top lower level and above)
- 15 min

**Cool-down:**

Slowly running around/loosening exercises

# Program 70

**2nd Competition Period**
**9th Week**

| TRAINING FEATURE | ORGANISATION/AMOUNT/TIPS |
|---|---|
| **Warm-up:**<br>Ball handling with changes of pace | • Trainer announces the pace, changes of direction and place.<br>• 15 min<br>• Stretching |
| **Technique:**<br>Individual techniques | • Ball control right and left<br>• Ball juggling with foot, knee, head, on the spot and moving<br>• Stopping the ball with chest, foot, thigh, on the spot and moving<br>• Shadow dribbling<br>• One partner dribbles ahead, the other imitates all his feints and deceptive manouevres.<br>• 15 min |
| Goal shot | • After a call from the trainer<br>• Two parties dribble all around a marked field until the trainer calls on a player to shoot at goal. This player must dribble through a marker mini-goal and immediately shoot at the main goal.<br>• 20 min |

**Fitness/Tactics:**

Forechecking

- Game 4:4:4 on half field
- Two teams A and B play against each other while team C waits outside the playing area until a goal has been scored. Then team C takes over from the scoring side. The team that lost the ball must move up to the center line to recapture the ball by "forechecking".
- 2 x/wk (medium level and above)
- 20 min

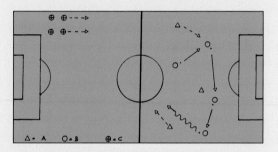

Closing game

- Game 11:11 (lower levels only)
- 25 min

- Game 8:8
- Two ball contacts/player
- 20 min

**Cool-down:**

Slowly running around/stretching

# Program 71

**2nd Competition Period**
**10th Week**

| TRAINING FEATURE | ORGANISATION/AMOUNT/TIPS |
|---|---|
| **Warm-up:**<br>Game 5:2 | • Two ball contacts/player<br>• Direct play<br>• 15 min<br>• Stretching |
| **Fitness:**<br>Acceleration speed | • Acceleration in a number of variations<br>• From a casual trot<br>• From a hop<br>• From a sideways gallop<br>• From walking on the heels<br>• From a skip<br>• From a slalom run<br>• All exercises can be carried out with an about turn.<br>• 2 x/wk (medium level and above)<br>• 2-3 series<br>• 3-5 min break between series |
| Ability to jump | • Resilience exercises for the leg muscles<br>• Jumping on one leg against resistance of partner |

- Jump and stretch up with partner's help

- Jumping down on steps

- Finishing jump with medicine ball

- Repeat each exercise 10 x
- 2-3 series
- Complete breaks between series

### Tactics:

Keeping the ball in own ranks

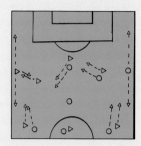

- Game 6:6 on half field
- Each team has starter player positioned on the sideline who trots up and down. Every pass to the starter player results in a point. The winner is the team with the most points.
- 2 x/wk (top lower level and above)
- 2 x 10 min with short break

### Variations:

Closing game

- Two ball contacts/player

- Game 11:11
- 25 min

### Cool-down:

Slowly running around

# Program 72

**2nd Competition Period**
**10th Week**

| TRAINING FEATURE | ORGANISATION/AMOUNT/TIPS |
|---|---|
| **Warm-up:** <br> Tiger ball 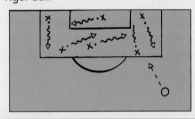 | • All players except one have a ball each and dribble across the penalty area. The "tiger" must try to capture a ball. Whoever loses his ball becomes the "tiger." <br> • 2 x 7 min with short break (stretching) |
| **Technique:** <br> Ball skills 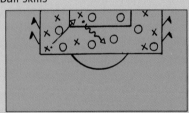 | • Game 8:8 in penalty area with two small goals <br> • The players dribble as much as possible to improve perfection with the ball (see Program 36). <br> • 2 x/wk (top lower level and above) <br> • 25 min |
| Goal shot | • Practicing freely – e.g after center passes, after corners, free kicks, penalties, etc. <br> • 20 min |
| **Fitness:** <br> Endurance specific to soccer | • Game 5:5:5 with small goals on half field <br> • One team always has a break and jogs around the playing field <br> • Stretching <br> • 10 min – then role swap <br> • 2 x/wk (medium level and above) |

**Tactics:**
Closing game

- 11:11
- 20 min

**Cool-down:**
Slowly running around

# Program 73

**2nd Competition Period**
**11th Week**

| TRAINING FEATURE | ORGANISATION/AMOUNT/TIPS |
|---|---|
| **Warm-up:**<br>Jogging and stretching | • 15 min |
| **Fitness:**<br>Speed with the ball | • 20 m sprints with the ball<br>• 10 x<br>• Keep the ball in the air for 30 s after each sprint<br>• Two series<br>• Complete break between series |
| **Technique:**<br>Dribbling<br><br>Goal shot | • Game 1:1:1<br>• One player has a break<br>• 3 min – then role swap<br>• 2-3 series<br>• Complete break between series<br>• Keep the ball in the air in groups of three<br><br>• After dribbling, 1:1 from center line:<br>• The defender runs from the sideline towards the player with the ball and attacks.<br>• 2 x/wk (medium level and above)<br>• 20 min |

**Tactics:**
Majority vs. minority

- Game 5:5 + one "neutral" on half field with small goals:
- The "neutral" always plays with the party in possession.
- 2 x/wk (medium level and above)
- 20 min

Closing game

- Game 8:8 on complete field
- 20 min (lower levels only)

**Cool-down:**
Loosening exercises

# Program 74

**2nd Competition Period**
**11th Week**

| TRAINING FEATURE | ORGANISATION/AMOUNT/TIPS |
|---|---|
| **Warm-up:**<br>Game 3:3 | • 15 min |
| **Technique:**<br>Individual techniques | • Each player occupies himself with his ball and trains his feeling for the ball as well as improving his ball skills.<br>• 15 min |
| Goal shot | • Practicing freely in groups<br>• 15-20 min |

**Tactics:**
Countering

- Game 7:7 on 3/4 field:
- Team A plays to two mini-goals (markers), team B plays to the main goal. If team A gets the ball it immediately tries to counter to the two mini-goals (confident through pass and fast free running).

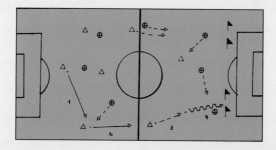

- After 10 min – role swap
- 2 x/wk (medium levels and above)
- 20 min

**Variation:**

- Game critique of last championship match
- Specific exercises to eradicate mistakes
- 20 min

**Fitness:**
Endurance

- 5,000 m run in 25 min "reminder strain" (see chapter 6)

**Cool-down:**
Stretching

# Program 75

**2nd Competition Period**
**12th Week**

| TRAINING FEATURE | ORGANISATION/AMOUNT/TIPS |
|---|---|
| **Warm-up:**<br>Game 5:2 | • Two ball contacts/player<br>• Direct play<br>• 15 min< |
| **Technique:**<br>Individual techniques<br><br> | • "Soccer tennis"<br>• Game 4:4 on marked field 15 x 15 m<br>• Net height 1.5 m<br><br>• One ball contact/player<br>• Three ball contacts/team<br><br>• As many ball contacts/player as desired; three ball contacts/team<br>• 20 min |
| **Variation:** | • As tournament with several teams |
| **Fitness:**<br>Acceleration speed | • Acceleration in a number of variations<br><br>• After keeping the ball in the air<br>• After brief passing play with partner<br>• After juggling ball while sitting<br>• After juggling ball with head<br>• After juggling ball with thigh<br><br>• 2-3 series<br>• 3-5 min breaks between series |

**Variation:**

- All accelerations without ball

**Tactics:**

Game overview and understanding of game

- Game 8:8 in a field divided 3/3
- In each third a certain way of playing the ball is allowed
- 1st field – free play
- 2nd field – two ball contacts/player
- 3rd field – direct play
- 2 x/wk (top/elite level)
- 20 min

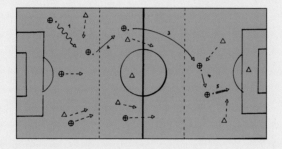

Closing game

- Game 11:11 with task: On losing the ball in the opponent's half immediately run back to the center line and occupy the appropriate spaces.
- 20 min

**Cool-down:**

Slowly running around

# Program 76

**2nd Competition Period**
**12th Week**

| TRAINING FEATURE | ORGANISATION/AMOUNT/TIPS |
|---|---|
| **Warm-up:**<br>Six day race<br>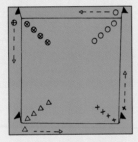 | • Four teams position themselves at the four corners of a rectangle. Atthe signal the first player of each team runs once around the rectangle and lines up at the back of his team; then the next one runs, etc.<br>• Running time 10 min<br>• The team that manages the most rounds in the given time wins. |
| Note:<br><br>Variation: | • Make sure the teams do not stand too close to the corners.<br>• With ball |
| **Technique:**<br>Free kick, corner, penalty | • Together with the trainer the players decides the strategies for carrying out the kicks.<br>• 2 x/wk (medium level and above)<br>• 20 min |
| **Fitness:**<br>Playing speed | • Game 6:6:6 on half field<br>• One team always has a break and stretches.<br>• Two ball contacts/player<br>• Direct play (medium level and above)<br>• Role swap after 15 min<br>• 45 min |

**Tactics:**
Game overview (peripheral view)

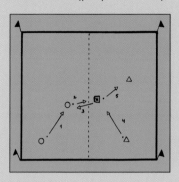

- Game 2:2 + one "neutral"
- The "neutral" moves between the two double pairs who must pass to him in alternation.
- The "neutral" must attentively observe the action so he is always ready to receive the ball (game maker function).
- 2 x/wk (top/elite level)
- 20 min

**Cool-down:**
Slowly running around

# Program 77

**2nd Competition Period**
**13th Week**

| TRAINING FEATURE | ORGANISATION/AMOUNT/TIPS |
|---|---|
| **Warm-up:**<br>Game 5:2 | • Two ball contacts/player<br>• Direct play<br>• 15 min<br>• Stretching |
| **Technique:**<br>Goal shot | • After bouncing off trainer |

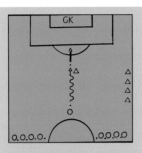

- After dribbling

- After high kick-off
- 20 min

**Fitness:**
Endurance specific to soccer

- Game 6:6 on half field
- Two ball contacts/player
- Direct play (top/elite level)
- Each team determines a "game maker" who may dribble and thus take the speed out of the game (mark him with a color).
- 20 min with short breaks

**Tactics:**
Pressing

- Game 5:5 on half field with small goals and the task: On losing the ball in the opponent's half all players move up and cover their man.
- If the party losing the ball outnumbers the others, two players go for the player with the ball.
- 2 x/wk (top lower level and above)
- 20 min

**Cool-down:**
Loosening exercises

# Program 78

**2nd Competition Period**
**13th Week**

| TRAINING FEATURE | ORGANISATION/AMOUNT/TIPS |
| --- | --- |
| **Warm-up:**<br>Running with changes of pace and direction | • Trainer announces how to run<br>• 15 min<br>• Stretching |
| **Technique:**<br>Individual techniques | • Each player occupies himself with his ball and works on his ball skills.<br>• 2 x/wk (top lower level and above)<br>• 15 min |
| **Fitness:**<br>Speed<br><br><br><br>Jumping endurance | • 30 m sprints<br>• 10 x – 30 s break between sprints<br>• Two series<br>• Complete break between series<br>• Jumps over a hurdle (25 cm high) with both legs<br>• Squat jump over tape<br>• Jumps to headers<br>• Partner holds the ball over his head.<br>• Each exercise two min long<br>• Two series<br>• Complete break between series |
| **Tactics:**<br>Preparation for next match | • Game and practice forms which cover the tactics of the coming match.<br>• 20 min |
| **Cool-down:**<br>Slowly running around | |

# Program 79

**2nd Competition Period**
**14th Week**

| TRAINING FEATURE | ORGANISATION/AMOUNT/TIPS |
|---|---|
| **Warm-up:**<br>Chain tag<br> | • All players in penalty area, which they may not leave. One "hunter" begins the game by trying to tag another. Once he has tagged one, together (hands linked) they go after the next, etc. Once a chain of four arises it is divided into two chains of two. The last untagged player is the winner.<br>• Several rounds<br>• 15 min<br>• Stretching |
| **Technique:**<br>Goal shot<br>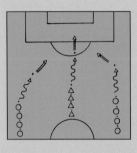 | • After dribbling from the center line:<br>• Three groups form up at the center line and head for the goal in turns, finishing with a shot at goal. |
| Variation: | • As above<br>• Goal shot after pass from trainer (pass across the field; the ball has to be run for)<br>• 20 min |

**Fitness:**
Speed endurance

- 3 x 4 accelerating runs diagonally across the field
- Start – acceleration – deceleration, recovery
- 3-5 min break between series, light ball work

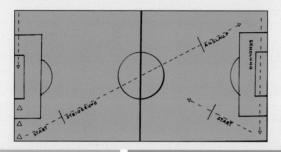

**Tactics:**
Covering the field

- Game 5:3 (see Program 38)
- 2 x/wk (medium level and above)
- 25 min

Closing game

- Game 11:11 with task: Goals from the "second row"
- 25 min (lower levels only)

**Cool-down:**
Walking around/stretching

# Program 80

**2nd Competition Period**
**14th Week**

| TRAINING FEATURE | ORGANISATION/AMOUNT/TIPS |
|---|---|
| **Warm-up:**<br>Game 5:2 | • Two ball contacts/player<br>• Direct play<br>• 15 min<br>• Stretching |
| **Technique:**<br>Individual techniques | • Dribbling with ball around slalom poles<br>• Play the ball high and stop it with the instep<br>• Play the ball high, stop it with the chest and move it on<br>• Juggle the ball with the foot and while running<br>• Play the ball back and forth between the feet while running forwards<br>• Play the ball forwards with the inside and pull it back with the sole (sole trick)<br>• Feint shot, but then take the ball away in a circle to left or right<br><br>• Repeat all exercises several times<br>• 15 min |
| Shield the ball<br><br><br><br>Variation: | • "Ball thief"<br>• All players are in a marked rectangle 10 x 10 m. The ball thief tries to get the ball of one of the players.<br>• Two players can function as "ball thief"<br>• 10 min |

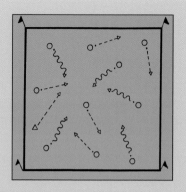

**Fitness:**
Speed with the ball

- 25 m sprints with ball
- 15 x – 30 s break between sprints

**Variation:**

- With about turn and 15 m sprint
- After throwing ball high, stopping it and sprinting
- From sitting and juggling on the instep

**Tactics:**
Playing on the wing

- Game 8:8 on whole field
- Task:
  The attacking team must play through one of the two mini-goals (markers, see Program 67) in order to score.
- 2 x/wk (medium level and above)
- 25 min

**Cool-down:**
Slowly running around

# Program 81

**2nd Competition Period**
**15th Week**

| TRAINING FEATURE | ORGANISATION/AMOUNT/TIPS |
|---|---|
| **Warm-up:**<br>Rope skipping/stretching | • Both legs without jump in between<br>• Both legs with jump in between<br>• One leg without jump in between<br>• One leg with jump in between<br>• Alternating jump left – right<br>• Running and hitting<br>• Stretching after each jumping form<br>• 15 min |
| **Technique:**<br>Individual techniques | • Ball control at top speed<br>• Two groups stand opposite each other on the penalty area line and the center line. At the whistle the groups exchange places. |
| **Variation:** | • At the midway point the players each give their ball to one of the other group.<br><br>• As above – with only one ball<br>• 15 min |
| **Goal shot** | • After dribbling in center circle |

- After running around in the center circle and a call from the trainer

**Variation:**

- As above
- The player called on does two push-ups before heading to the ball.

- 20 min

**Tactics/Fitness:**
Securing the ball

- Game 6:6 on half field with the task: In one's own half the ball may only be dribbled, in the opponent's half only two ball contacts are allowed.
- 2 x/wk (top lower level and above)
- 25 min

**Cool-down:**
Slowly running around

# Program 82

**2nd Competition Period**
**15th Week**

| TRAINING FEATURE | ORGANISATION/AMOUNT/TIPS |
|---|---|
| **Warm-up:**<br>Jogging and stretching | • 15 min |
| **Technique/Fitness:**<br>One on one training | • Game 1:1 |

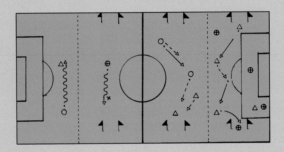

• Game 1:1 with small goals (goal scores possible from in front and behind)

• Game 2:2 with small goals (goal scores possible from in front and behind)

• Game 4:4 with small goals (goal scores possible from in front and behind)

• 3-5 min
• 2-3 series
• Complete breaks between series
• 2 x/wk /top/elite level)

**Tactics:**

Corner with extension

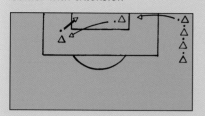

- The corners are kicked to the shorter post, where a team-mate stands, who passes the ball on with head or foot.
- Corners from right and left
- 2 x/wk (medium level and above)

Closing game

- Game 11:11
- 25 min

**Cool-down:**

Slowly running around

# Program 83

**2nd Competition Period
16th Week**

| TRAINING FEATURE | ORGANISATION/AMOUNT/TIPS |
| --- | --- |
| **Warm-up:**<br>Combination in penalty area | • Playing together in pairs in penalty area<br>• Trainer gives instructions on changes in pace and direction.<br>• 15 min<br>• Stretching |
| **Fitness:**<br>Jumping ability, leg power, speed endurance | • Circuit training with five stations<br>**1st Station**<br>Flat passes over 15 m<br><br>**2nd Station**<br>Header pass while jumping |

**3rd Station**
Game 1:1

**4th Station**
Medicine ball throw in over 5 m

**5th Station**
Rope skipping

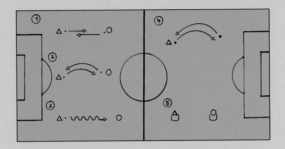

- Two partners always practice together, two have a break.

- 2 min/station
  Break: 2 min/station
- 2-3 series
- Complete break between series – light ball work

**Technique:**
Goal shot

- Practicing freely
- 20 min

**Tactics:**
Covering the field

- Game 6:6 on half field with small goals with the task: On losing the ball in the opponent's half immediately run back to the predetermined space.
- 2 x/wk (medium level and above)
- 20 min

**Cool-down:**
Slowly running around/stretching

# Program 84

**2nd Competition Period**
**16th Week**

| TRAINING FEATURE | ORGANISATION/AMOUNT/TIPS |
|---|---|
| **Warm-up:**<br>Scuffle ball with medicine ball | • Two teams with five to eight players try to carry a medicine ball across the goal line with fast direct passing amongst themselves. The physical activity may only be directed at the ball, not at other players (see Program 49).<br>• 15 min |
| **Technique:**<br>Individual techniques<br><br><br><br>**Variation:** | • Game 3:3 with small goals and the task: The ball may only be played with the "weak" foot, otherwise it changes possession.<br>• 2 x/wk (medium level and above)<br>• 30 min<br>• After 10 min the teams swap players. |
| **Fitness:**<br>Acceleration speed | • Acceleration in a number of variations (see Program 75) |
| **Tactics:**<br>Getting behind the defense<br><br><br>Closing game | • Game 5:5 on half field (see Program 16)<br>• 2 x/wk (top/elite level)<br>• 25 min<br>• Game 11:11<br>• 25 min |
| **Cool-down:**<br>Slowly running around | |

# Program 85

**Transitional Period**
**1st Week**

| TRAINING FEATURE | ORGANISATION/AMOUNT/TIPS |
|---|---|
| **Warm-up:**<br>Handball game<br>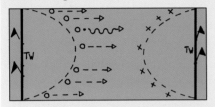 | • Played according to handball rules in penalty area with small goals (3 m)<br>• 15-20 min |
| **Technique:**<br>Individual techniques | • "Soccer tennis" (see Program 58)<br>• With several teams as a tournament<br>• Playing time 10 min – then change<br>• 2 x/wk (top lower level and above) |
| **Fitness:**<br>Endurance specific to soccer | • Game 6:6 on half field<br>• Two ball contacts/player<br>• Direct play (medium level and above)<br>• 2 x/wk (medium level and above)<br>• 3 x 15 min with short breaks<br>• Stretching |
| **Tactics:**<br>Playing for goal opportunities<br> | • Game 5:4 with main goal<br>• After each goal or gaining of possession by the defense the next attack begins at the center line.<br>• 2 x/wk (medium level and above) |

| Variation: | • Group of five: two ball contacts/player<br>• Group of two: free play<br>• 25 min with role swap |
|---|---|

**Cool-down:**
Slowly running around

# Program 86

**Transitional Period**
**1st Week**

| TRAINING FEATURE | ORGANISATION/AMOUNT/TIPS |
|---|---|
| **Warm-up:**<br>Game 5:2 | • Two ball contacts<br>• Direct play<br>• 15 min |
| **Technique:**<br>Goal shot | • After center pass from right and left – two players stand as attacking forwards in the penalty area while the rest form up on the center line. The first player of the group dribbles past slalom poles to the goal out line and plays a center pass or a back pass to the two forwards who must score a goal. |
| Variation: | • With three forwards and two defenders<br>• 2 x/wk (medium level and above)<br>• 25 min |

**Fitness/Tactics:**

Covering the field

- Game 8:8 with the task:
  On losing the ball in the opponent's half all players must run back to their own half as quickly as possible and take up their positions.
- 3 x 15 min with role swap within the 8 men teams

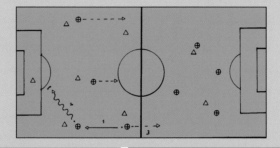

**Cool-down:**

Slowly running around/stretching

# Program 87

**Transitional Period**
**2nd Week**

| TRAINING FEATURE | ORGANISATION/AMOUNT/TIPS |
|---|---|
| **Warm-up:**<br>Trotting with changes of pace | • Trainer gives instructions on how to run, e.g one field length slowly<br>half a length medium<br>half a length slowly<br>a length medium<br>half a length slowly<br>half a length quickly<br>• 5-7 series with short breaks |
| **Variation:** | • With ball |

**Technique:**

Individual techniques

- Each player occupies himself with his own ball
- 15 min

Corner, free kick, penalty

- Practicing freely
- 2 x/wk (medium level and above)
- 25 min

**Tactics/Fitness:**

One on one training

- Game 6:6 on half field: Each player must cover a certain player when the opposing team has the ball (close covering).

**Variation:**

- Each player covers the opposing player closest to him (short running distances).

- Two ball contacts/player
- Direct play (top/elite level)
- 2 x/wk (top/elite level)
- 3 x 15 min with short breaks – stretching

**Cool-down:**

Slowly running around/loosening exercises

# Program 88

**Transitional Period**
**2nd Week**

| TRAINING FEATURE | ORGANISATION/AMOUNT/TIPS |
|---|---|
| **Warm-up:**<br>Game 5:2 | • Two ball contacts<br>• Direct play<br>• 20 min |
| **Technique:**<br>Goal shot<br> | • After pass and 1.1:<br>Both partners start at the trainer's signal and must fight for the ball. Whichever gets to the ball first can shoot at goal. |
| **Variation:** | • After the start both players must jump over a hurdle. |
| Goal shot | • After heading duel 1:1<br>Trainer throws a ball between the players who have their backs to the goal. Whichever one gets the ball under control first can take a shot.<br>• 2 x/wk (medium level and above)<br>• 25 min |
| **Tactics/Fitness:**<br>Endurance specific to soccer | • Game 5:5 on half field with small goals<br>• Two ball contacts (top lower level and above)<br>• Free play (lower levels) |

- The teams swap players amongst each other.
- 35 min

**Cool-down:**
Walking around/slowly running around

# Program 89

**Transitional Period**
**3rd Week**

| TRAINING FEATURE | ORGANISATION/AMOUNT/TIPS |
| --- | --- |
| **Warm-up:**<br>Game 3:1 | • Two ball contacts<br>• Direct play<br>• 15 min |
| **Technique:**<br>Individual techniques | • Turning kick from the hip right and left: Three players stand 5 m apart. The middle player has the ball thrown to him and carries out turning kicks from the hip alternating right and left.<br>• Role swap |

- Header: Two partners take turns at throwing each other the ball and jumping to head it back.
- 2 x/wk (top lower level and above)
- 25 min

**Tactics/Fitness:**
Majority vs. minority

- Game 5:5 + two "neutrals" who always play with the team in possession.

- Each player is a "neutral" once.

**Variation:**

- With small goals
- Two ball contacts/player
- 2 x/wk (top/elite level)
- 3 x 10 min with short breaks

- Stretching

**Cool-down:**
Slowly running around

# Program 90

**Transitional Period**
**3rd Week**

| TRAINING FEATURE | ORGANISATION/AMOUNT/TIPS |
|---|---|
| **Warm-up:**<br>Jogging and stretching | • 15 min |
| **Technique:**<br>Goal shot  | • After pass and call from trainer: Three players run up and down on the level of the penalty area until the trainer calls on them one after another to shoot. |
| Variation: | • Slow pace<br>• Medium pace<br>• Fast pace<br>• 2 x/wk (medium level and above) |
| Heading | • Trainer throws an attacker the ball to head past a defender to the goal.<br>• 30 min |

**Tactics/Fitness:**
Securing the ball

- Game 11:11 with the task: On gaining the ball the team now with the ball tries to reduce the pace of the game by combining as safely as possible in its "own ranks" (direct passes and majority at the ball).
- 35 min

**Cool-down:**
Loosening exercises

# Program 91

**Transitional Period**
**4th Week**

| TRAINING FEATURE | ORGANISATION/AMOUNT/TIPS |
|---|---|
| **Warm-up:**<br>Game 5:2 | - Two ball contacts<br>- Direct play<br>- 20 min<br>- Stretching |
| **Technique:**<br>Individual techniques | - Each player occupies himself with his ball.<br>- 15 min |

**Fitness:**
Strength, jumping ability, jumping strength

- Partner exercises

- Heading duel – one player bounces the ball on the ground; both jump to head it.

- While running the partners pull each other forward, first one then the other (linked hands).

- Piggyback partner

- Jump from a low crouch with partner's help.

- Two players carry a third

- All exercises are carried out several times.

**Tactics:**
Game without ball

- Game 6:6 on half field with small goals
- Two ball contacts/player
- 2 x/wk (medium level and above)
- 25 min

**Cool-down:**
Slowly running around

# Program 92

**Transitional Period**
**4th Week**

| TRAINING FEATURE | ORGANISATION/AMOUNT/TIPS |
|---|---|
| **Warm-up:**<br>Running and stretching | • Trainer determines a player who carries out the warm-up. |
| **Variations:** | • In groups the players warm-up on their own.<br>• 15 min |
| **Technique:**<br>Individual techniques | • "Soccer tennis" (see Program 85)<br>• 20 min |
| **Fitness:**<br>Acceleration speed | • Acceleration in a number of variations<br>• From a sitting position<br>• From lying on the stomach<br>• From lying on the side<br>• From a kneeling position (sprinter start)<br>• From sitting with crossed legs<br>• From a one-armed press-up<br>• Five series<br>• 3-5 min break between series |
| **Variation:** | • All accelerations with ball |
| **Tactics:**<br>Shifting the game | • Game 7:7 + two "neutrals" on field between the two penalty areas (see Program 46)<br>• 25 min |
| **Cool-down:**<br>Slowly running around | |

# Program 93

**Transitional Period**
**5th Week**

| TRAINING FEATURE | ORGANISATION/AMOUNT/TIPS |
|---|---|
| **Warm-up:**<br>Game 3:1 | • Two ball contacts/player<br>• Direct play<br>• 15 min<br>• Stretching |
| **Technique:**<br>Dribbling<br> | • Dribbling against two players one behind the other<br>• Five dribblings/player then roleswap<br>• 2-3 series<br>• Complete break between series |
| **Variation:**<br>Flat pass and header<br> | • Dribbling to the goal<br>• Three players stand in a row, the player in the middle must in turn quickly return a flat pass and a header to the passer.<br>• 3 min fast pace<br>• Then role swap, 2-3 series<br>• Complete breaks between series, light ball work<br>• 2 x/wk (medium level and above)<br>• 25 min |
| **Tactics/Fitness:**<br>Playing for goal opportunities | • Game 6:6:6 on whole field:<br>• Team A is positioned 10 m in front of its own goal; team B on the other side of |

the playing field while team C stands between both. Team C starts an attack on team A and tries to score a goal. If a goal is scored or the ball lost the teams exchange roles and team A plays against team B, etc.

- 2 x/wk (medium level and above)
- 35 min

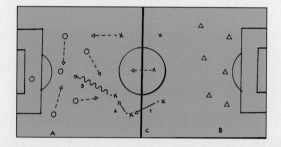

**Cool-down:**
Slowly running around

# Program 94

**Transitional Period**
**5th Week**

| TRAINING FEATURE | ORGANISATION/AMOUNT/TIPS |
|---|---|
| **Warm-up:**<br>Game 5:2 | • Two ball contacts/player<br>• Direct play<br>• Stretching<br>• 20 min |
| **Technique:**<br>Goal shot<br> | • After through pass from the center line<br><br>• Lob after through pass from center line<br><br>• After back pass from goal out line<br>• Two partners continually pass each other the ball from the center line in the direction of the goal until one of the two runs to the goal out line and plays a back pass to the player who held back, who must immediately shoot at goal. |

- Practice from right and left
- 2 x/wk (medium level and above)
- 25-30 min

**Tactics/Fitness:**
Playing speed

- Game 6:6 on half field
- Two ball contacts/player
- Direct play (top lower level and above)
- 2 x/wk (medium level and above)
- 2 x 12 min with short break

Closing game

- 11:11
- 20 min

**Cool-down:**
Slowly running around

# Program 95

**Transitional Period**
**6th Week**

| TRAINING FEATURE | ORGANISATION/AMOUNT/TIPS |
|---|---|
| **Warm-up:**<br>Jogging and stretching | • 15 min |
| **Technique:**<br>Flat pass from a turn<br>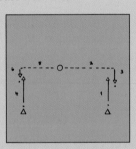 | • On receiving a pass from two team-mates the third must run after the ball and play it back after turning.<br><br>• 3 min fast pace – then swap roles<br>• Two series<br>• Complete break between series, light ball work |
| Header from a turn<br>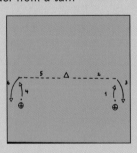 | • As above – but with header from a turn<br>• 3 min fast pace – then role swap<br><br>• Two series<br>• Complete break between series, light ball work<br>• 25-30 min |
| **Tactics/Fitness:**<br>Game without ball | • Game 7:7 on 3/4 field<br>• Two ball contacts/player<br>• Direct play<br>• 3 x 10 min with short breaks – stretching |
| **Cool-down:**<br>Slowly running around | |

# Program 96

**Transitional Period**
**6th Week**

| TRAINING FEATURE | ORGANISATION/AMOUNT/TIPS |
|---|---|
| **Warm-up:**<br>Game 5:2 | • Two ball contacts/player<br>• Direct play<br>• 15 min |
| **Technique:**<br>Goal shot | • Practicing freely<br>• 20 min |
| **Tactics/Fitness:**<br>Game creativity | • Game 4:4 with small goals<br>• In tournament form with teams changing amongst each other<br>• 2 x/wk (medium level and above)<br>• 35 min with short breaks<br><br>• 11:11<br>• 35 min (lower levels) |
| **Cool-down:**<br>Slowly running around/walking around | |

# 11 Training in Halls and Fitness Studios

The winter months are a difficult time for the amateur field. On the one hand there may be a winterbreak, on the other hand though there are still championship matches and training in bad weather conditions.

Many trainers are therefore faced with the question of whether they should rather cancel trainings, which is certainly the worst solution, or whether they should move them into a hall.

Training runs after dark are also not exactly the ideal solution. To keep up team spirits and keep the loss of fitness to a minimum many trainers decide to transfer training notice to a hall at short.

The writer himself is opposed to halls, but nevertheless wishes to offer the user the possibility of carrying out training that is at least a little more attractive.

The fact is that the attendance suddenly increases when training is moved indoors. The reasons are obvious and well-known. Because players in the hall mostly want to get playing, it is best to satisfy this desire as quickly as possible.

With so-called **circuit programs** the trainer can motivate the players to "voluntarily" do something to keep up their fitness.

The circuit programs have the advantage that many players can practice at the same time. Groups of four are ideal, in which two players practice and two take a break.

Before the players go through the program they should be well warmed-up and have done stretching exercises.

With the help of the circuit programs the trainer can measure performance capacity by having players note their results on test cards.

The length of the exercises, the breaks and the number of rounds for the program are indicated.

# Circuit Program Tailored to Soccer

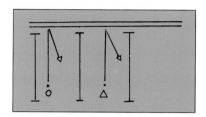

### Station 1
"Squash soccer"
- Double pass with wall and two benches
- The ball may only be played at the wall from a spot marked on the floor.

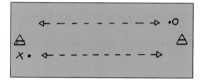

### Station 2
Slalom
- Dribble past six markers 2.5 m apart

### Station 3
Sprint with the ball
- 10 m sprint with ball and back

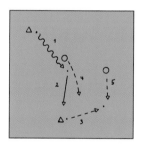

### Station 4
Game 2:2
- Without goals
- With goals

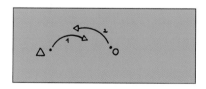

### Station 5
Heading
- Heading from jump after ball is thrown

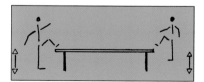

### Station 6
Step jumping
- Alternating with right and left foot, jump onto a small box, etc.

| | |
|---|---|
| **Strain:** | 60 s |
| **Break:** | 60 s |
| **Series:** | 3-5 |
| **Breaks between series:** | Complete |

**Material:**
Eighteen markers, nine balls, a small box or crate, three benches on their sides, a stopwatch, six numbered station cards.

# Training in the Fitness Studio

Training in the fitness studio gives players the opportunity to build up their muscles again after a long injury break. Especially after operations, it is advisable to carry out rehabilitation training in consultation with a doctor.
This training has the advantage that targeted muscle training can restore sporting form more quickly.

Training with the equipment should be done under supervision of a qualified sport or fitness teacher.

The well-known system **S – S – S** (stretching – strengthening – stretching) should be followed.

**S** –Stretching exercises prepare the muscles for the strain, improve circulation and extend agility. They also serve the athlete as a self-test of whether the muscles are in a pain free condition.
**S** –Strengthening exercises improve neuro-muscular performance capacity and encourage growth of the trained muscles as well as removing the muscular deficit of the operated joints or muscle groups involved.
**S** –Stretching exercises directly after strengthening remove contraction residues of the strengthened muscles, reduce the degree of tension and contribute to more mobility in the joints. Furthermore the general capacity for regeneration is improved and the training effect increased.

For strength training we do not offer a complete program but restrict ourselves entirely to the muscle system to be strengthened.

When training with equipment certain criteria should be adhered to.

- Choose a controlled, dynamic pace of movement.
- Pay attention to correct breathing when pulling or pressing.
- Avoid over-stretching joints.
- Make sure the vertebrae (spinal column) are straight.
- Carry out 10-15 repeats per series.
- Do 2-4 series on each device.

The degree of intensity of the exercises can be decided on using the RPE scale (Rate of Perceived Exertion), which indicates the subjectively felt degree of exertion.

**RPE Scale**

(Borg 1970, in E. TRUNZ/I. FREIWALD/P. KONRAD 1992 – Fit durch Muskeltraining)

| | |
|---|---|
| 6 | |
| 7 | ultra light |
| 8 | |
| 9 | very light |
| 10 | |
| 11 | quite light |
| 12 | |
| 13 | somewhat strenuous |
| 14 | |
| 15 | strenuous |
| 16 | |
| 17 | very strenuous |
| 18 | |
| 19 | |
| 20 | ultra strenuous |

The above figures stand for the number of repeats of each exercise.

### 1. Leg bender, lying

Muscles trained: Rear thigh muscles, calf muscles

**Comment:**
- Avoid hollow back by contracting stomach muscles or lying on a pad
- Eyes down
- Do not completely stretch knee joints in returning phase.

### 2. Leg stretcher

Muscles trained: Front thigh muscles (four headed knee joint extensor)

**Comment:**
- Keep back straight
- Movement as far as stretching the knee joint
- Variation – with one leg

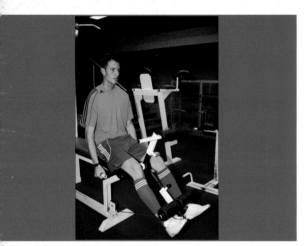

### 3. Calf muscles, standing

Muscles trained: Twin calf muscles, M. soleus, foot muscles, toe bending muscles

**Comment:**
- Stand with feet at hip width
- Stabilise hip, back and shoulder muscle systems
- Look ahead
- Maximum stretching of the feet

### 4. Leg adductor, sitting

Muscles trained: Thigh contractors (leg adductors)

**Comment:**
- Back straight against the rest
- Look straight ahead
- Press the upper pads together
- Variation – with legs stretched

### 5. Leg abductor, sitting

Muscles trained: Thigh opening muscles (leg abductors)

**Comment:**
- Press back straight against the rest
- Look straight ahead
- Press the upper pads apart
- Variation – with legs stretched

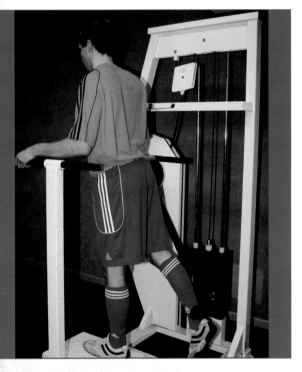

## 6. Hip pendulum buttocks training

Muscles trained: Large gluteal muscle, rear thigh muscles, lower back extensor muscles

**Comment:**
- Bring hip joint into position as extension of the device's axis
- Look straight ahead
- Contract rump muscles
- Return stretched leg, over stretching in hip joint to a maximum of 15°.

## 7. Buttocks trainer, lying

Muscles trained: Large gluteal muscle, lower back stretching muscles

**Comment:**
- Bring hip joint into position as extension of the device's axis.
- Push down pads by stretching in hip joint, over stretching in hip joint to maximum 15°.

### 8. Knee bending with dumb-bell

Muscles trained: Front thigh muscles, large gluteal muscle, rear thigh muscles, calf muscles

Comment:
- Dumb-bell pole a little more than shoulder width
- Feet shoulder wide – toes slightly outwards
- Rise from 90° to stand and go down again.

### 9. Stomach muscle trainer, lying

Muscles trained: Straight inner and outer oblique stomach muscles, hip bending muscles

Comment:
- Bend legs to c. 90°
- Roll up upper body so that the lumbar vertebra is still lying
- Look obliquely upwards
- Variation – when rolling up turn upper body across (oblique stomach muscles).

### 10. Raise thighs

Muscles trained: Front thigh muscles, arm, shoulder and rump muscles

Comment:
- Lower arms rest on the pads
- Back presses straight against the rest
- Raise thigh to 90° position and lower again.

### 11. Back stretcher, lying

Muscles trained: Complete neck and back extensor muscle systems, large gluteal muscle, rear thigh muscles

Comment:
- On stomach, pelvic rim lies on pad
- Hands behind neck, elbows at shoulder level
- Upper body at an angle
- Roll up upper body to a horizontal position (do not over stretch).

### 12. Latissimus-pull

Muscles trained: Broad back muscle, large and small round muscle, biceps, inner arm bender, upper arm spoke muscle, chest muscles

Comment:
- Straight back
- Legs in 90° position
- Hold at a little more than shoulder width
- Pull pole down to neck level.

### 13. Bench pressing, sitting

Muscles trained: Chest muscles, triceps, front M. seratus anterior, delta muscle

Comment:
- Back straight
- Hands wider than shoulder width
- Press away from the chest
- Hands wide apart (emphasis on chest muscles)
- Hands closer together (emphasis on triceps).

### 14. Biceps Curl

Muscles trained: Double headed arm bender (biceps), inner arm bender, upper arm spoke muscle

**Comment:**
- Upper arms rest on Curl platform
- Hold grips at shoulder width
- Movement as far as maximum bending of elbow joint
- In the return phase no complete stretching in the elbow joints.

### 15. Bicycle ergometer

Training effect: Heart-circulatory system, thigh and calf muscles

**Comment:**
- Adjust saddle height so that when the pedals are vertical the leg is still slightly bent
- Wattage adjustable from 50 Watt to 200 watt
- This device can also be used for warm-up.

# 12 Appendix – Stretching

Stretching as a warm-up or cool-down exercise has taken its place firmly in the training schedule. Here we demonstrate 25 different exercises which cover a broad spectrum of stretching and relaxing exercises.

Underlying considerations regarding stretching:

- Regular stretching relaxes body and mind.

- Stretching reduces muscle tension (a pre-stretched muscle can take more).

- Stretching improves muscle coordination and eases carrying out of movements.

- Stretching prevents muscle damage such as pulling and tearing, etc.

- Stretching stimulates the heart and circulatory system.

- Stretching contributes to faster regeneration after sporting strain.

Proper stretching must be learned. Slow and continuous stretching is the best way to bring the muscle to its final position. Here one must take note that the muscle should be lightly pre-stretched at the beginning (c. 10-20 seconds). Afterwards increasing stretching is carried out.

The so-called stretch reflex protects muscles from overexertion and injuries. If the muscles are stretched too quickly and jerkily this can cause minor injuries (microtraumas) and the actual effect is lost.

Stretching is directed concretely against the stretch reflex. It improves muscle tone. The stretch reflex remains limited exclusively to the stretched muscle and does not extend to neighbouring muscles.

The exercises are divided according to the four functional circles of KNEBEL (in: Frank, G.: Fußball – Konditionsgymnastik, Frankfurt/Berlin 1994), see Fig. 4.

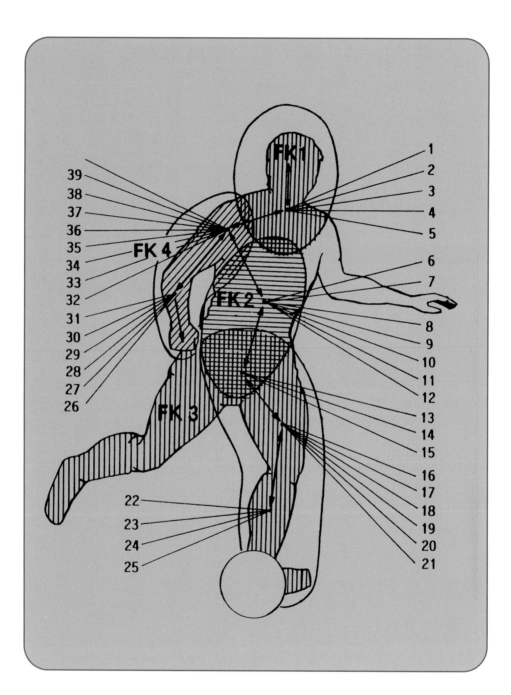

*Fig. 4: The four functional circles (FK)*
*(Source: FRANK, G.: Fußball – Konditionsgymnastik, Frankfurt / M. / Berlin, 1994)*

1   Head turner (m. sternocleidomastoid)
2   Hood muscle (m. trapezius)
3   Shoulderblade lifter (m. levator scapula)
4   Head of the longest back muscle (m. longissimus capitis)
5   Deep muscles of the neck vertebrae
6   Straight stomach muscle (m. rectus abdominal)
7   Oblique stomach muscle (m. oblique abdominal)
8   Horizontal stomach muscle (m. transverse abdominal)
9   Longest back muscle (m. longissimus dorsi)
10 Back extensor (m. erector spinae)
11 Deep muscles of the spinal column
12 Serratus anterior (serratus anterior)
13 Back extensor (m. sacrospinalis)
14 Trunk flexor (m. iliopsoas)
15 Gluteal muscle (m. gluteus maximus)
16 Thigh contractor (m. tensor fascia lata)
17 Tailor muscle (m. sartorius)
18 Leg adductor (adductors)
19 Leg abductor (abductors)
20 Four headed knee joint extensor (m. quadriceps)
21 Knee flexor – hamstrings (m. ischiocrurales)
22 Toe extensor (m. extensor digitorum longus)
23 Toe flexor (m. flexor digitorum longus)
24 Muscles of the upper ankle joint (dorsal-/plantar flexors)
25 Muscles of the lower ankle joint (pronators/supinators)
26 Finger flexor superficial (m. flexor digitorum superficialis)
27 Finger flexor deep (m. flexor digitorum profundus)
28 Finger extensor (m. extensor digitorum communis)
29 Thumb muscles (extensors, flexors, adductors and abductors)
30 Wrist flexor and extensor (m. flexor resp. extensor carpi radialis und ulnaris)
31 Upper arm muscle (m. brachioradialis)
32 Double headed elbow extensor (m. biceps brachii)
33 Triple headed elbow flexor (m. triceps brachii)
34 Inner arm muscle (m. brachialis)
35 Medial and lateral rotators (pronators and supinators)
36 Chest muscles (m. pectoralis major and minor)
37 Shoulder muscles (m. deltoid)
38 Broadest back muscle (m. latissimus dorsi)
39 Scapula muscles (m. teres major and minor)
40 Supra and infraspinatus (m. supra and infra spinam)

### Functional Circle 1

Neck vertebrae with head and chest vertebrae to the fifth chest vertebra

**E-1**

On back, legs bent, hands behind neck, slowly roll up upper body.

**E-2**

Standing with feet at shoulder width, left hand takes right hand and draws it slowly obliquely downwards, slowly turn head to left.

### Functional Circle 2

Chest vertebrae from fifth to twelfth chest vertebra, loins, pelvis, hip area

**E-3**

Sit, clasp knees with both hands and slowly pull towards chest.

**E-4**

On back, bend knees and clap with both hands, slowly roll up body.

**E-5**

Kneeling, slowly lean back on the lower legs and support with hands behind buttocks.

**Functional Circle 3**

Lower vertebrae, hip joint, sacrum and ilium (haunch bone) joint, complete lower extremities

**E-6**

Kneeling, place the toes of one foot level with the knee of the other leg, push upper body slightly forwards.

**E-7**

Extended step forward until one lower leg is in the vertical, the knee of the other leg touches the ground, slowly lower the hips.

**E-8**

Extended step forward until one lower leg is in the vertical, bend the back knee and pull the foot further inwards (right angle), move shoulder away from lowered knee and support with hand beneath leg, slowly lower hips.

**E-9**
Extended step forward, bend one leg and grasp ankle with hand, slowly lower hips and pull heel to middle of buttocks.

**E-10**
Sit, place soles of feet against each other, slowly draw them forwards from the hips.

**E-11**
One leg in front at goal post, front leg bent, back leg stretched, slowly move hips forward, heel of back leg remains on ground.

**E-12**
Stretching seated position, one leg bent, move foot sole of bent leg to knee of stretched leg, slowly move upper body forwards.

**E-13**

Lying on back, bring foot soles together and slowly draw heels towards buttocks.

**E-14**

Lying on back, clasp one knee and pull it up upper body towards opposite shoulder.

**E-15**

Crouch, feet flat on ground (turned c. 15° outwards), keep knees outside shoulder breadth, heels 10 to 30 cm apart.

**E-16**

Put foot on railing, step etc., bend knee of raised leg and slowly move hips forwards.

**E-17**

Lying on back, one arm spread sidewards, lay one leg at a right angle on the other side and slowly press down the knee with the other hand.

**E-18**

Standing crouch, place hands on ground, stretch one leg sidewards.

**E-19**

Standing, clasp ankle slowly pull lower leg towards upper leg.

**E-20**

Stand at shoulder breadth with balls of feet on edge of step (partner holds hands firmly), slowly lower heels.

**E-21**

Lying on back, with both hands clasp the back of the knee of one leg and pull it towards the upper body.

**E-22**

Standing with legs at shoulder breadth with shoulder towards goal post or similar. Stretch out arm and clasp post, slowly turn head and look back over the other shoulder.

**E-23**

Standing with legs at shoulder breadth, fold hands, turn palms outwards and stretch arms in the horizontal.

**E-24**

Standing with legs at shoulder breadth, fold hands, turn palms outwards and stretch arms vertically over head.

**E-25**

Standing with legs at shoulder breadth, one hand reaches for the opposite shoulder, the other hand reaches for the elbow and slowly pushes the arm downwards.

## Photo & Illustration Credits

Cover Photo:      dpa Picture-Alliance
Cover Design:     Jens Vogelsang
Inside Photos:    Gerhard Frank
Illustrations:    Gerhard Frank

## SOCCER ALIVE
### THE GAME IS THE BEST TEACHER

- New training philosophy
- Train as if in a real game situation
- Become a smart player

D. BRUEGGEMANN

MEYER & MEYER SPORT

## SOCCER INJURIES
### PREVENTION AND TREATMENT

- Protect your valuable legs
- Modern treatments for soccer-specific injuries
- Get back to the game in no time

MEIER · SCHUR, MD

MEYER & MEYER SPORT

---

D. Brueggemann
**Soccer Alive – The Game is the Best Teacher**

Soccer is a game that requires the player to be quick not only in movement but also in decision-making. Everyday soccer training focuses on improving technical and tactical abilities and almost completely neglects to emphasize the importance of being able to read the game and to make the right decision quickly. Soccer Alive presents the new didactical approach of using game situations to improve movement and behavior. Coaches and parents of anyone from recreational level to high school level and beyond will benefit from this book.

192 pages, full-color print
196 photos, 114 illustrations
Paperback, 6 $^1/2$" x 9 $^1/4$"
ISBN: 978-1-84126-235-2
$ 19.95 US
£ 12.95 UK/€ 19.95

Ralf Meier/Andreas Schur, MD
**Soccer Injuries**

At both grass-roots and major league levels, soccer players' legs are both precious and injury-prone items. One false step, tiredness, lack of concentration or a rough tackle are all it takes to overstrain muscles and tendons, leading to week-long lay-offs from training and matches. Trainers, physical therapists, coaches and physicians work together to keep these injury breaks as short as possible. This book describes modern methods of treatment for soccer-specific injuries and shows how training can be better structured to try to avoid risk factors in the future.

128 pages, full-color print
32 photos & 6 illustrations
Paperback, 6 1/2" x 9 1/4"
ISBN: 978-1-84126-237-6
$ 16.95 US
£ 12.95 UK/€ 16.95

MEYER & MEYER SPORT

# The Sports Publisher

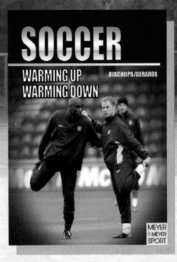

**Ralf Meier**
**Strength Training for Soccer**

Muscle tears, tendon and joint injuries belong to soccer like studs to soccer shoes. Many of these injuries are preventable, in particular by better preparation of the leg muscles. Functional strength training prepares the muscles specifically for the demands of soccer. Match-fit muscles not only make you a better player, they are also the best way of protecting tendons and joints. This book has exercises to train the soccer player's most important muscles and also to improve flexibility and joint mobility.

128 pages, full-color print
100 photos
Paperback, $6^1/2$" x $9^1/4$"
ISBN: 978-1-84126-208-6
$ 16.95 US
£ 12.95 UK/€ 16.95

**Bischops/Gerards**
**Soccer – Warming up and Warming down**

In this book the authors provide some 35 programs for proper warming-up and warming-down for soccer. The programs are full of variety to avoid monotony and are based around the game of soccer itself, within a team situation. The book proceeds from a basic understanding of the needs of every individual to stretch and ease their muscles and tendons, through a series of simple games and exercises using the football and other aids.

**2nd edition**
136 pages, two-color print,
22 photos, 172 figures
Paperback, $5^3/4$" x $8^1/4$"
ISBN: 978-1-84126-135-5
$ 14.95 US
£ 8.95 UK/€ 14.90

# www.m-m-sports.com

MEYER
& MEYER
SPORT

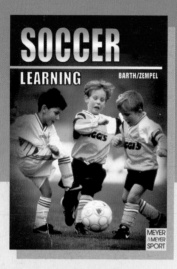

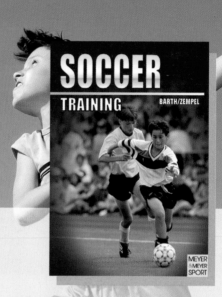

Barth/Zempel
**Learning Soccer**

Billy, "the magic mouse," ac-companies children through the book, and talks about all you need to know about soccer. It answers questions on soccer gear, regulations, soccer clubs, the history of soccer, and everything else children are interested in, to become a celebrated "magic mouse" some day. Basic techniques are explained so they are easily understood, and suggestions are made to promote independent practice.

Barth/Zempel
**Training Soccer**

Your child wants to get serious about soccer training – but what's the best approach? This book endeavors to answer that question in a manner to which children can readily respond. A training companion and workbook in one, it takes up where "Learning Soccer" leaves off. Readers additionally receive excellent, challenging and age-appropriate information covering a full range of topics including physical condition, mental preparation, etc.

136 pages
Full-color print, some photos numerous drawings
Paperback, 5³/4" x 8¹/4"
ISBN: 978-1-84126-130-0
$ 14.95 US
£ 9.95 UK/€ 14.90

152 pages
Full-color print, some photos numerous drawings
Paperback, 5³/4" x 8¹/4"
ISBN: 978-1-84126-131-7
$ 14.95 US
£ 9.95 UK/€ 14.90

© kristian sekulic/fotolia.com